NOT BY FAITH ONLY

MESSIANIC JEWISH DISCIPLESHIP
FROM THE BOOK OF יעקב YA'AQOV (JAMES)

KEVIN GEOFFREY

©2023 by Kevin Geoffrey

All rights reserved. Except for brief quotations for the purpose of review or comment, or as quotations in another work when full attribution is given, no part of this book may be reproduced, stored in a retrieval system, or transmitted in any form or by any means—electronic, mechanical, photocopy, recording or otherwise—without the prior permission of the publisher.

A ministry of Perfect Word Ministries

www.perfectword.org
1-888-321-PWMI

Scripture quotations are from the Messianic Jewish Literal Translation of the New Covenant Scriptures (MJLT NCS).

ISBN #: 978-0-9837263-6-4

Cover art by Esther Geoffrey
Photo by Yevhen Polishko/123RF

Printed in the United States of America

To Hosea

Some common sense teaching
for an uncommon young man
and the grown man you are quickly becoming.

You are pleasing in your father's sight.
I love you.

Special thanks to all the generous and faithful friends and partners of Perfect Word and MJMI, our board members, and especially my family, for all your love, prayers and support. Thank you for helping me continue to teach and proclaim the truth of God's word.

Contents

Introduction vii
  Chapter 1: Count It All Joy 1
  Chapter 2: Doubting Nothing 6
  Chapter 3: Humble Exaltation 11
  Chapter 4: Why Bad Things Happen 16
  Chapter 5: The Father Brought You Forth for a Reason 21
  Chapter 6: God's Righteousness and Being Slow to Anger 26
  Chapter 7: Receive the Word, Then Do It! 31
  Chapter 8: Devotion Pure and Undefiled 36
  Chapter 9: Bringing the King's Torah to Its Goal 41
  Chapter 10: The Torah of Liberty—So Speak, and So Do 46
  Chapter 11: Not By Faith Only 51
  Chapter 12: For We All Make Many Stumbles 56
  Chapter 13: The Tongue: World of the Unrighteousness 61
  Chapter 14: The Tongue's Deadly Poison 66
  Chapter 15: Who Among You Is Wise and Understanding? ... 71
  Chapter 16: You Receive Not, Because You Ask Evilly 76
  Chapter 17: Friendship Is Hostility 81
  Chapter 18: Be Submitted and He Will Exalt You 86
  Chapter 19: Speak Not, Judge Not, Do Not 91
  Chapter 20: If the Master Wants, We Will Live 96
  Chapter 21: Do Good, or It Is Sin 101
  Chapter 22: You Stored Up Treasure 106
  Chapter 23: Be Patient and Stabilize Your Heart 111
  Chapter 24: Thou Shalt Not Grumble 116
  Chapter 25: Let Your Yes Be Yes 121
  Chapter 26: You Are Not Alone 126
  Chapter 27: That You May Be Healed 131
  Chapter 28: Going Astray From the Truth 136
Glossary of Hebrew Terms 143
About the Author 145

Introduction

MY INITIAL EXPERIENCE WITH THE BIBLE was not a normal one. At eighteen years old, when I first became a believer in Jesus, I used to read the Bible constantly. But having no previous experience with the Book (and being at that time alone in my faith, with no one around to instruct me), I didn't know that the Gospels—the records of Yeshua's life and teachings—should have held more interest to me than they did. For some reason, it would be quite a while before I would read even a single one of those accounts all the way through. Instead, I found myself returning, over and over again, to the book of James.

Despite this unusual approach to the Bible, I don't think it was in any way detrimental. On the contrary, though Yeshua remained a bit hazy to me for a little while longer, what I found by concentrating on James (who is, in actuality, Jacob or יַעֲקֹב, Ya'aqov) was surely formative, not just to my outlook on the faith, but to my eventual approach as a teacher of the Scriptures. In a sense, I had merely skipped to the end, and discovered a crucial point that so many followers of Messiah seem to miss. And that is, that our righteousness in Yeshua is declared not by faith alone, because that faith must be perfected by putting it into action. In short, what we *believe* is supposed to determine what we *do*.

I therefore regard my early focus on Ya'aqov as providential, since it has never been an issue for me to balance faith with actions. I have never been confused, thinking that the way we behave (a.k.a. "works") could ever earn us favor with God. And, at the same time, I have had no problem accepting that faith without actions, as Ya'aqov says, is dead. Where many have perceived tension between faith and actions, I have always found harmony—the first leading naturally into the second; the latter, in turn, building up the former. But more importantly, Ya'aqov taught me that belief, while fully sufficient for salvation, is by itself *insufficient* for an effective, daily walk in the Master.

The reason I so dearly love the book of Ya'aqov—one of the most overlooked books of the Bible—is because it is Messianic Jewish discipleship at its finest. While in many ways its instructions are a hodgepodge of topics (much like the Torah which Ya'aqov himself regarded so highly), it offers sage, spiritual, and—most of all—practical guidance that leads us into maturity and helps us to persevere in our lives as Messiah-followers. Within the chronology of Scripture, Ya'aqov wrote his letter over a decade before Paul ever put pen to paper. He was writing in the wake of a period of extreme persecution of the early Messianic Jewish community, an oppression which left them dispersed throughout the ancient world (Ya'aqov 1:1, cf. Acts 11:19). And it was in this context that Ya'aqov wrote on such ordinary topics as interpersonal conflict, how to deal with anger, how to handle wealth, and how to plan for the future. But he also wrote on subjects of deep, eternal import—things that can easily be shaken during difficult and trying circumstances—such as how to endure the testing of our faith, how to overcome the persistent temptation of sin, how to be patient in suffering, and how to remain true to God in a world hell-bent on making us His enemy.

Not By Faith Only, then, is my effort to expound upon this invaluable and timeless centerpiece of practical instruction for our faith in Yeshua. This book contains nearly the entirety of Ya'aqov's letter (exceptions made only for brevity) based on the text of the *Messianic Jewish Literal Translation of the New Covenant Scriptures (MJLT NCS)*. In each short chapter, I walk you through a subsequent portion of Ya'aqov's letter, elaborating and teaching on the subject of his instruction. Then, in keeping with the spirit of discipleship, the body of each chapter is followed by a series of questions for your self-reflection or group discussion, and ends with a closing prayer.

The questions have been designed to help you not only grasp the main points of each chapter, but then put the word of God into practice in your life. Some questions are of a factual nature, and while you are certainly free to explore whatever thoughts these questions prompt in your mind, our goal and hope is that, before doing this, you will first go back to the chapter and Scripture to the find the answers. In addition to this type of review question, there are also questions with personal application in mind. Your responses to these will, of course, be unique to you. Each multi-part question generally yields separate answers for its individual parts; however, it is more than appropriate to write a single answer that considers all the parts together. And to ensure that the questions would be helpful and effective, they have each been field-tested and fully approved by the whole Geoffrey Family, with my deepest gratitude to my wife Esther for the time and tremendous work that she invested in the questions' development. Finally, the prayer after the questions is there to help you ask God for the ability to apply what you learned in the chapter, and to have those truths sealed and reinforced in your heart and mind.

The title *Not By Faith Only* comes from יַעֲקֹב Ya'aqov 2:24, which perfectly sums up both the content and character of his letter. It speaks to the way Ya'aqov continually encourages us to stay grounded in a useful faith, while urging us to take actions that are natural extensions of it. Ya'aqov models a perfect cooperation between the believing and the doing—teaching us as Yeshua's disciples how we must excel at both if we are to succeed at either.

As you read and interact with *Not By Faith Only*, I pray that it will spur you to begin pushing your faith a bit further out into the world so that your actions can make a difference in the lives of others. May you find *Not By Faith Only* a worthy and edifying exploration—both of the letter from the brother of the Messiah, and of yourself.

In Yeshua's eternal service,

Kevin Geoffrey
May 16, 2023

NOT BY FAITH ONLY

MESSIANIC JEWISH DISCIPLESHIP
FROM THE BOOK OF יעקב YA'AQOV (JAMES)

Chapter 1

Count It All Joy

> *From* יַעֲקֹב, Ya'aqov, a slave of God and of the Master יֵשׁוּעַ, Yeshua *the* Messiah; to the Twelve Tribes *of Yis'rael* who are in the Dispersion: שָׁלוֹם, Shalom. Count *it* all joy, my brothers, when you fall into various *ways of* testing, knowing that the proving of your faith brings about perseverance *in you*. And let the perseverance have a maturing work, so that you may be mature and complete, lacking in nothing.
>
> יַעֲקֹב *YA'AQOV 1:1-4 (MJLT)*

YA'AQOV HAD EVERY RIGHT TO BRAG. Being the brother of Yeshua, he also garnered a great deal of respect and influence as an authoritative voice among the Emissaries. And yet, when he wrote his powerful letter to the Jewish believers *"who* had been scattered abroad from the oppression that came after Stephen" (Acts 11:19, MJLT), he identified himself in his greeting simply as "a slave of God and of the Master יֵשׁוּעַ, Yeshua *the* Messiah." More than a mere statement of humility, acknowledging one's position as a "slave" emphasizes and elevates the position of one's "Master." It speaks categorically as to whose purpose one will serve, and whose desires one will subvert. It is from this lowly vantage point that Ya'aqov is fully qualified to address the plight of his brothers and sisters, and to advise them in their behavior and actions as they live their own lives as slaves of Messiah.

It was the oppression of Ya'aqov's fellow Messianic Jews—their being persecuted and scattered for their belief in Yeshua as Messiah—that caused Ya'aqov to begin his letter with the famous exhortation to "count *it* all joy." It dramatically changes our understanding of Ya'aqov's words when we realize that the "various *ways of* testing"—the "testing" which Ya'aqov is encouraging his readers to consider as joy—are a direct result of their dispersion from their homeland at the hands of their own unbelieving Jewish family. What could be a greater source of depression and fear than to be so harshly rejected by one's own people? And yet, this is Ya'aqov's entire point. Though they had had to flee to safety for fear of retribution, imprisonment, or worse, everything they endured was for "the proving of [their] faith," and by knowing this, it would "bring about perseverance" in them. God's tests show us what our faith is made of, and from that faith, we may find the joy to persevere.

There is a reason for God's people to persevere with joy—to struggle and press through in the face of adversity—especially in times that our safety is threatened and our faith is challenged. It is to "let the perseverance have a maturing work, so that [we] may be mature and complete, lacking in nothing." Though it is easier said than done, we persevere for the same reason that Ya'aqov exhorted those early Jewish believers to persevere: at the end of all the running is the destination God has planned for you. The end-goal of the Messianic faith, then, is not persecution and adversity; rather, the adversity is what prepares us to fully and effectively live out our Messianic faith. Ya'aqov wants his readers to be "mature and complete, lacking in nothing" in spite of what the persecution and adversity have already taken away. As disciples of Messiah, we need to learn to live with nothing but our burning passion for serving Yeshua, so that even in the worst of circumstances, we will never go without.

And this brings us back to joy.

An immature, incomplete follower of Messiah will take the safe route and avoid adversity, and he might even feel happy... for a time. But the mature Messiah-follower will put his faith even above safety and comfort, and when he sees how triumphantly he perseveres, he will consider the times of testing a joy to him. He will see God's hand. He will see God's faithfulness. He will see how enduring hardship for the sake of the Messiah pleases the Master he serves and readies him to fulfill his purpose as Yeshua's disciple.

Let us not wait until we are under grave oppression before we consider various ways of testing as tremendous times of joy. Every day, in far less severe ways, we have the opportunity to practice finding that joy—so do it! Our God has a destination in mind for you, and when you arrive, he wants you fully grown, lacking in nothing, and ready.

QUESTIONS

Chapter 1

1. Ya'aqov saw himself first and foremost as "a slave of God and of the Master Yeshua *the* Messiah." In what areas of your life have you fully submitted yourself to God? In what areas do you need to make your own will submit to the Master's?

2. Ya'aqov was writing to believers who had been scattered abroad, been rejected by their families, and faced much persecution. In your own life, what circumstances are testing your faith? How often do you find joy in and through those trials?

3. We are encouraged to embrace testing with joy, because our perseverance increases as our faith is proven. How have you

seen your faith proven in the past? What trials do you need to stop avoiding now so that your perseverance can grow?

4. According to Ya'aqov, the ultimate goal of our trials is to make us "mature and complete, lacking in nothing." How has your character grown and matured during previous times of testing? In what areas is your character still lacking?

PRAYER

Master Yeshua, I am Your humble slave; I exalt Your great and mighty Name! Prepare my heart for what lies ahead, so that in all things I may be ready to persevere and endure. Test me, ADONAI, and prove me; show me the way to a faith that is far greater than my fear. I bless Your Name, O God, Savior of my soul. Mature me and make me complete, so that no matter what ways of testing may come, I will faithfully count it all joy.

Chapter 2

Doubting Nothing

> And if any of you lacks wisdom, let him ask from God —who is giving to all, generously and not denouncing— and it will be given to him; and let him ask in faith, doubting nothing. For he who is doubting has been like a wave of the sea, driven by wind and tossed *about*. For let not that man suppose that he will receive anything from the Master—a two-minded man *is* unstable in all his ways.
>
> יַעֲקֹב YA'AQOV 1:5-8 (MJLT)

W*HEN WE FIND OURSELVES FACING* difficult and trying times, it's easy to lose our heads. The brain shuts off, the fear ramps up, and calm, rational decision-making is replaced by emotional, knee-jerk reactions to people and circumstances. Without even realizing it, we are consumed with every negative thought and event, oblivious to the storm inside our minds that we ourselves created through our own poor choices and wrong actions. Not only are we unable to find a way out, but we are past the point of remembering even to look for one. We're stranded, lost, and hopeless—caught inside our own instability.

So when times of testing come unexpectedly barrelling upon us, the better course would be to immediately admit our own shortcoming—and, yes, the overwhelming tendency toward total *stupidity*—and instead, ask God to give us *wisdom*. "And if any of you lacks wisdom, let him ask from God—who is giving to all, generously and not denouncing—and it will be given to him." Wisdom for good decision making, wisdom for how to constructively persevere through hard times, wisdom for allowing the teaching hand of God to lead us into maturity—all this wisdom and more is available to us if we will simply remember to ask. God will not "denounce" us, finding us to be weak and incompetent. Not at all. Rather, when we admit our "lack," He responds with generosity, providing all the wisdom we need to meet the troubles we will encounter.

The key to successful receipt of this outpouring of wisdom, however, is to "ask in faith, doubting nothing. For he who is doubting has been like a wave of the sea, driven by wind and tossed *about*." When we doubt that God has enough wisdom to pass on to us, we revert to our default setting of being "driven by wind and tossed *about*" by every emotion and circumstance that slams against our bow. Instead, we should be "doubting nothing"—especially not God's ability to provide us with unending wisdom.

We must not doubt that the wisdom of God is enough to guide us through choppy waters. We must not doubt that, through Yeshua, we can persevere and endure the storm. We must not doubt that we will lack nothing we truly need as long as we place our trust in God's generous willingness to save.

When we doubt that God will answer us when we ask, we cut ourselves off from securing the strengthening we need, and the results are devastating. As the storm rages, life throws as much at us as it can, causing us to be swiftly overwhelmed and filled with doubt. Then—unless we are quick to push aside that doubt and look to Yeshua, so as to receive strengthening from the Father—the doubt overtakes us, and we are easily swept away. Indeed, for the one who doubts, "let not that man suppose that he will receive anything from the Master." If we trust more in our own abilities than in God's, we block anything and everything that God has ever wanted to give us. Then, when we—being consumed with doubt—try later to ask for help, He cannot give it, and we are left on our own. We have defeated ourselves.

God does not want us eternally torn between two minds: ours and His. "A two-minded man *is* unstable in all his ways." If we are constantly trying to balance how much we can take upon ourselves with how much help we need to ask of God, we will be hopelessly unsteady in everything. When difficult times arise, there is no better first thought than to accept that it's entirely out of your hands, and then to ask God for all wisdom, "doubting nothing." We only hurt ourselves when we make it difficult for God to give us what we need; indeed, we will only find stability when we stop depending on ourselves.

QUESTIONS

Chapter 2

1. Times of testing often reveal our shortcomings, as emotions and fears begin to affect our judgment. In what types of situations do you rely on your own wisdom to save you? How can you remember to immediately ask for God's wisdom when trials come?

2. Ya'aqov promises that if we "ask in faith, doubting nothing," God will generously give us wisdom. Why is it so important to ask God for wisdom when we are surrounded by confusion and chaos? How much confidence do you have that He will give you wisdom when you ask for it?

3. A doubting person is compared to "a wave of the sea, driven by the wind and tossed *about*." Why does doubt make us so

unstable? What are some ways that you can stop your doubts before they have a chance to take root?

4. According to Ya'aqov, a double-minded man is unstable, and will not "receive anything from the Master." How have you been torn between depending on yourself and depending on God? In what areas or situations do you need to stabilize yourself so that you can receive wisdom from the Master?

PRAYER

ADONAI, my God, You are awesome and mighty to save. In the midst of the storm of my mind, Father, I call out to You for Your peace and perfect wisdom. Help me, Abba, to be full of faith, even as the chaos and uncertainty swirl around me. I praise You, Master, that You do not denounce me in my time of need, but instead stabilize my trust, that I may rely completely on You—doubting nothing.

Chapter 3

Humble Exaltation

> And let the brother who is humble take pride in his exaltation, and the *one who is* rich, in his humiliation, because, as a flower of grass, he will pass away. For *as* the sun rises with the burning heat, and THE GRASS WITHERS, AND THE FLOWER OF IT FALLS, and the beauty of its appearance is destroyed, so also the rich *man* in his pursuits will fade away! Happy *is* the man who perseveres *through the ways of* testing, because, becoming proven *in his faith*, he will receive the crown of the Life, which the Master promised to those loving Him.
>
> יַעֲקֹב *YA'AQOV 1:9-12 (MJLT)*

FROM THE MOMENT THAT MANKIND BECAME capable of accumulating wealth, there have existed the extremes of those who abound in material riches, and those who have little to none. While this outward inequality may seem to some an immoral injustice, to others it is no more than natural economic reality. Many, in the hopes of doing good, may seek to relieve the plight of the poor—some through voluntary charity, others by forceful rule of law. But in Messiah, all who are wealthy and all who go without will become equalized—not in the things we have, but in the character of who we are.

The way in which this equalization is accomplished appears, at first blush, contradictory, as it runs opposite to what we would normally expect. Nevertheless, "let the brother who is humble take pride in his exaltation, and the *one who is* rich, in his humiliation." To suggest that someone who is "humble" ought to "take pride" in anything seems initially counterintuitive. But this particular "pride" is the kind that allows the humble brother to accept his reality in Messiah, which is, *exalted*. At the same time, while one might expect a rich person to already be full of *selfish* pride, he is nonetheless to "take pride" as well—not in his wealth, status, or success, but in the reality of his *humiliation*.

But why would a rich person be *humiliated?* "[B]ecause, as a flower of grass, he will pass away." Though we may normally associate wealth with prestige, privilege, and perhaps even a greater responsibility to society at large, the rich one is also at a disadvantage to "the brother who is humble," since, as he seeks to retain and grow his wealth, eventually, "the rich *man* in his pursuits will fade away!" Every beautiful and precious thing he owns will ultimately be destroyed, and, in the end, while all his material possessions are being burned in the fire, the light of destruction will only serve to illumine his humiliation.

Does this mean that it is wrong to be rich? Not at all. It only means that, in Messiah, "the *one who is* rich [ought to take pride] in his humiliation." In other words, just as the humble brother can accept his exalted reality in Messiah, the rich brother can accept his *humiliation* in Messiah. Through Yeshua, both men find their value—not in the things they have, nor in the things they lack, but in their equal and shared pursuit of God.

And what of the humble brother? How can his lack be reason for exaltation? "Happy *is* the man who perseveres *through the ways of* testing, because, becoming proven *in his faith*, he will receive the crown of the Life, which the Master promised to those loving Him." Perseverance proves faith, which crowns the humble brother with Life.

Though ways of testing have served to destroy many a man, we as Messiah's disciples can find happiness in it—as long as we persevere. Whether we are rich or humble, perseverance produces happiness in us because our self-worth and inner spirit are elevated as we endure in Messiah, ultimately leading to eternal Life. By pressing on in the face of adversity, we prove—to God, but especially to ourselves—that our faith is stronger than any inherent, situational, or imagined weakness. By enduring times of testing, we humble ourselves only to be further exalted, as we demonstrate the reality of our trust and hope in God.

Today is the day for you to humbly persevere and prove your faith, so that you "will receive the crown of the Life, which the Master promised to those loving Him." To live forever, then, in the presence of Yeshua—this is the greatest (and most humbling) exaltation of them all.

QUESTIONS

Chapter 3

1. Inequalities between rich and poor are a perpetual reality in this world. In Messiah, how does finding our value in our shared pursuit of God equalize these differences? At the end of this life, what humiliation will come to the rich, and what exaltation awaits all who persevere with faith?

2. Ya'aqov says that we are like "a flower of grass" and "will fade away." Besides material possessions, which of your pursuits and achievements will ultimately have no value? In what areas of your life have you been finding your worth in things that are not eternal?

3. Times of testing are difficult to endure, yet we can find happiness through them. What character trait is necessary in or-

der to find happiness as you experience testing? How has perseverance through ways of testing, or a lack of it, proven the quality of your faith?

4. "The crown of the Life" will be given to all those who love the Master and faithfully persevere. Describe the encouragement you receive from this promise as you endure the ways of testing. Compared to the exaltations of this world, how much value should you place in being exalted by the Master?

PRAYER

Creator and Taker of life, I stand in awe of Your unlimited power. You alone raise up and tear down; You choose whom to elevate and whom to humble. As I bow myself before You, Master, I receive my undeserved exaltation, and I persevere toward my eternal crown. In both poverty and wealth, ADONAI, test me and find me faithful, that my sole pursuit in life will only ever be You.

Chapter 4

Why Bad Things Happen

> Let no one being tempted say, "I am tempted from God," for God is not tempted by evil, and *so He* Himself tempts no one. Rather, each one is tempted, being led away and enticed by his own desires. Afterward, the desire (having conceived) gives birth to sin, and the sin (having become fully-grown) brings forth death. Be not led astray, my beloved brothers!
>
> יַעֲקֹב *YA'AQOV 1:13-16 (MJLT)*

BAD THINGS HAPPEN ALL THE TIME. They happen to "bad" people as much as they happen to "good" ones. So when bad things happen, it's natural for us to wonder, "Why, God? Why did You allow this bad thing to happen to me?" It's not a rebellious thought; it's a question. It's seeking to know what is quite often unknowable. Yet questioning this way has the potential to become extremely problematic, as it can lead to accusation. "I thought You were a loving God! A loving God would never allow a bad thing to happen, so this bad thing is Your fault, God! Or, maybe, You don't even exist at all!" And down the slippery slope we go. When we reach this point, though, it's not because we don't understand God; it's because we don't understand the consequences of sin, and how sin works.

When the very first bad thing in all of history happened, it wasn't because of God (see Romans 5:12). It started with one man and one woman's *temptation*. But "no one being tempted [may] say, 'I am tempted from God,' for God is not tempted by evil, and *so He* Himself tempts no one." Enter: an external stimuli, a stray thought, an outside voice telling a person he can have something he shouldn't... and in that moment lies the opportunity to choose. This is temptation. It is the same process that happens every day with every one of us. But it's what happens next that really matters.

"Rather, each one is tempted, being led away and enticed by his own desires." So, it is not by God's efforts *but our own desires* that we are enticed to do wrong. At the moment our desires become activated by the temptation, we have not yet sinned, but there remains only an instant to choose whether we will turn away from it, or grant our desires the permission and power to lead us.

And then, once we have relinquished our conscience's authority, "afterward, the desire (having conceived) gives birth to sin, and the sin (having become fully-grown) brings forth death." Like a wanton woman inviting impregnation, desire resides within us, awaiting temptation's overture. Then, from the moment the two unite, sin is conceived within us—our own desire giving it life.

From this point on, sin can do nothing but grow out of control—clouding our judgment, rendering reason and warnings useless, becoming increasingly impossible to eradicate. And save the intervention of Yeshua through the Ruach HaQodesh (Holy Spirit), we will remain at sin's mercy until it is done having its way with us. Then, when sin becomes its own full-grown, monstrous being—ravaging and destroying our lives from the inside—"sin… brings forth death." We become an empty, unredeemable husk, suffering the eternal consequences of our lustful choices.

Bad things do not happen because God is unloving, or unfit, or unable, or unalive. So why, then, do bad things happen? Because we leave the door open to temptation, desire, sin, and death. Not only are we directly impacted by our own poor decisions and moral failings, as well as the errors and choices of those around us, but even where "bad things" like disease and disaster are concerned, our responses can mean the difference between life or death.

Though we may still sometimes ask God, "Why?" yet never be given an answer, one thing is for sure: the "bad thing" of sin and death that affects every one of us is not God's fault; it is ours… and it is unfair to expect Him to put a stop to something that we ourselves have set in motion. It is time to stop living obliviously and unaware regarding our desires, and instead admit our weaknesses and prepare ourselves to resist temptation by enacting God's Word in our lives. We need to guard against the lure of our desires before our actions force us to bear the consequences of our self-wrought sin. "Be not led astray, my beloved brothers!"

QUESTIONS

Chapter 4

1. Too often, we blame God when bad things happen to us, even when they are really the consequence of our own sin. In your life, what bad things have happened that were caused by your wrong responses to temptation? According to Ya'aqov, what is the sequence of events leading from temptation to death?

2. When we face temptation and our desires are stirred, there is only an instant to choose which path we will take. In that moment, how can you respond to your fleshly desires so that you will not sin? If you have already started down the path that leads to death, what do you need to do?

3. Some bad things happen to us simply because the world is broken, marred by sin from the very beginning. Explain how your response to this type of bad thing (i.e. disease, disaster)

can mean the difference between life and death. When faced with tragedy, how can you resist the temptation to blame God and lose faith?

4. Now is the time to admit our weaknesses and prepare ourselves to resist temptation. In what areas of your life are your desires most likely to lead you astray? What things should you be doing now so that you will be prepared to avoid and resist temptation?

PRAYER

Great and mighty, compassionate God, I admit to You my weakness! Forgive me, Master, for ever accusing You of causing the consequences of my own permissiveness toward sin. Help me, Father, to turn away quickly from temptation—to choose to follow Your word instead of my own selfish and fleshly desires. Thank You, Abba, for enduring my doubts about Your intentions, and for teaching me to resist the "bad things" of my heart.

Chapter 5

The Father Brought You Forth for a Reason

> Every good *act of* giving, and every perfect gift, is from above, coming down from the Father of the lights, with whom is no variation or turning shadows. Having *so* intended, He brought us forth with a word of truth, for us to be a certain *kind of* first-fruit of His created *things*.
>
> <div dir="rtl">יַעֲקֹב</div> YA'AQOV 1:17-18 (MJLT)

FAR TOO MANY OF TODAY's followers of Messiah are plagued by a tendency toward self. In many quarters, what currently passes for a gathering of sincere believers is, in actuality, just a biblically-laced, motivational-speaker-led self-help seminar. Whether the auditorium seats fifty, five hundred, or five thousand, too many of us continue seeking and coming back for these existential encounters because they shroud our own self-oriented motives under a spiritual-ish garment—and we believe we are benefitting and growing from what we are being fed. No one can fault a disciple of Messiah who desperately desires to find spiritual health and wholeness, but—believe it or not—a sense of well-being or self-worth, while important, is *not* the goal of our faith in Messiah. No, the purpose of your life in Yeshua is far greater than you realize.

When we focus too much on ourselves and our own needs, we naturally become takers and consumers. This not only feeds our spiritual unhealthiness and general ineffectiveness for Yeshua, but short-circuits our ability to become conduits for the outpouring of God's gifts to the world. Paradoxically, our wholeness is not solely dependent upon what we nourish ourselves with, but how we *selflessly* give of ourselves to others. Our orientation, then, should not be one of a taker, but a giver—one who gives abundantly of himself, knowing that he is giving the gift of God.

When we give, then, as disciples of Messiah, "Every good *act of* giving, and every perfect gift, is from above, coming down from the Father of the lights." While the taker in us wants to give with selfish motives—to feel good about ourselves, to curry favor, to gain influence—we are instead supposed to recognize that if the gift is indeed good and perfect, then it actually doesn't come from us. As Messiah-followers, we are mere caretakers—we're just the delivery guy—and it is the Father Himself who is the original sender. And because it is "coming down... from above," no earthly gift can ever compare. Every dollar, euro, yen, and shekel in the world pales in the splendor of the gift given "from the Father of the lights."

We know that such giving is good and perfect because "with [the Father there] is no variation or turning shadows." His light is brilliant and pure. His way is straight and level. He does not promise, then waver; He does not offer, then withhold. If the Giver and the Gift share these unbending, uncompromising qualities, how much more are we beholden to the very same goodness and perfection in our giving. Only in this way can the recipient be certain of the nature of the gift, and receive it in confidence and awe. Only in this way can we be trusted as the intermediaries of such a divine transaction.

This is why, "[h]aving *so* intended, He brought us forth with a word of truth." We cannot be authentic representatives of Messiah while we are consuming the spiritually evocative and the Scripturally deficient, all in pursuit of personal betterment or supernatural experience. The "word of truth" says that any inward focus must eventually turn outward.

The reason the Father has brought us forth, then, is not so that we can be happy, or safe, or mended, or fulfilled. No, we have been brought forth "for us to be a certain *kind of* first-fruit of His created *things.*" God has done something miraculous for you that He wants to do for others *through you.* Anything that the Master grants to you is ultimately in support of this singular goal. When He fixes you, it is so that you, in turn, can take part in fixing others.

As those who are "first"—going before all those who are yet to believe—we, the disciples of Messiah, have an unmitigated responsibility to put ourselves *last.* Our mandate is clear: to represent God and His interests by freely and selflessly giving of ourselves, and by faithfully delivering His gifts—unadulterated—to the world.

QUESTIONS

Chapter 5

1. Describe how a religious event could be closer to a motivational-speaker-led self-help seminar than to a biblical gathering of believers. Spiritual health and wholeness are necessary, but what happens when you make your own well-being the goal of your faith?

2. In Yeshua, we have a perfect model of how to be a giver and not a taker. In what ways, both physically and spiritually, do you regularly give to others—from your family members, to people you don't even know? In what ways do you focus more on what you can take for yourself than on what you can give?

3. Ya'aqov tells us that "every perfect gift is from above, coming down from the Father of the lights." What good and perfect

gifts has the Father given to you? What is the greatest of those gifts? How well are you passing on the Father's gifts to others?

4. Since God "brought us forth with a word of truth, for us to be a certain *kind of* first-fruit," what responsibility has He then given to us? How does consuming the spiritually evocative and the Scripturally deficient hinder us from fulfilling that responsibility?

PRAYER

Father in Heaven, I have been misfocused—searching for spiritual wholeness, while settling for self-help. Teach me, Abba, to find my sense of self-worth not just in what I receive from You, but in what I abundantly give out to others. Reorient me, ADONAI, and make me a selfless giver of Your glorious, perfect gift—giving with only pure motives. Bring me forth, Master, to be a certain kind of first-fruit who faithfully bears Your word of truth.

Chapter 6

God's Righteousness and Being Slow to Anger

> Know *this*, my beloved brothers, and let every man be swift to hear, slow to speak, *and* slow to anger, for the anger of a man does not accomplish the righteousness of God.
>
> יַעֲקֹב *YA'AQOV 1:19-20 (MJLT)*

HAVE YOU EVER HAD THAT FEELING during an intensely heated argument or disagreement when your vision starts to narrow, you begin to actually feel the inside of your ears start to close up, your face and body grow conspicuously hot, and you get the sensation of being surrounded—closed in, trapped—while the pressure inside of you keeps mounting and swelling and building and magnifying until it seems like your head is about to implode?

For those of us fortunate enough to be unfamiliar with this experience, that lovely feeling is what's known in certain circles as *anger*—that strong, volatile emotion some of us get when we believe that we've been seriously wronged.

It's interesting that, as our anger escalates, it can manifest itself in such a physical, palpable way. That closing up of the ears is more than just a telltale sign that we're filling with rage; it's just plain ironic. When we become angry, the one thing that would be most helpful in defusing the situation is often the first thing to go: our hearing. It's not that we lose the ability to distinguish sounds, but we instead become *deaf* to what the other person is saying. We stop listening, or worse, start filtering everything the other person says through our anger. This causes us to mishear or misinterpret things in a way that they aren't actually said or meant. This is why, when we begin to get angry, we first need to force ourselves to become "swift to hear." Only with this first step will love, patience, and sometimes even reality, begin to prevail.

But that is only the beginning of Ya'aqov's practical instruction, because unless we are also "slow to speak," we will be unable to stop the death spiral of anger from continuing. Being "slow to speak," then, allows us to take full advantage of our ears while they are still open. By giving the other person a chance to talk and express themselves, we have the opportunity to quietly and calmly listen to their words and weigh their thoughts—to truly listen to the heart of what is being communicated. When we are "slow to speak," we aren't calculating our next scathing point in our heads as we wait impatiently for the other person to make the stupid mistake of... pausing. Rather, we should be purposely holding our tongues and stilling our minds until the other person has finished their thought, and *then* when it is appropriate to respond, we can do so deliberately, carefully and compassionately.

These two sides of anger management—being "swift to hear" and "slow to speak"—will always result in one being "slow to anger." It is important to recognize, however, that it does not say, "do not ever get angry." We should be reminded of our Master Yeshua, and how He reacted when some people challenged His teaching as an excuse to make accusations against Him. The Scriptures say that He looked upon them with *anger* (see Mark 3:1-5). This shows us that even the perfect One can have a normal, natural anger response to a wrong being done. But the issue is not so much whether or not we get angry in the first place, but rather what we are angry about, and what we will do with that anger once it begins to percolate. Do we restrain it, even channel it constructively, and allow it to be tempered by the Spirit? Or do we let it flail out of control—our wrath unleashed in a violent fury? For what it's worth, the Scriptures say that the Master's anger was mixed with *grief*. One would think that had an effect.

In the end, every time our anger is selfish, self-oriented, and sustained by rage, it "does not accomplish the righteousness of God." When we start to get those physical cues that the anger is rolling in, "the righteousness of God" says we are to calm down, count the other person higher than ourselves, unclog our ears, and stop up our mouths. God's righteousness doesn't care how badly we've been wronged... it only minds how justly we respond.

QUESTIONS

Chapter 6

1. When our anger is stirred, being "swift to hear" is the complete opposite of our natural inclination. In the middle of a heated argument, why is it so easy for us to misunderstand what the other person is saying? If we are "swift to hear" in such situations, what effect will it have?

2. We cannot truly be "swift to hear" if we are not also "slow to speak." Why do so many of us feel the need to immediately express our own thoughts or opinions when disagreement or conflict arises? How does being "slow to speak" help us keep our anger from spiraling out of control?

3. How is being "slow to anger" different from simply bottling anger up inside, waiting until it eventually builds to the point that we erupt? In your own life, what is your typical response

to perceived wrongs, and how, if at all, does that response need to change?

4. When we look at the life of Yeshua, our perfect standard for righteousness, we see times when He became angry. In what situations is it not only okay, but righteous, to be angry? In such circumstances, how, if it all, does that change our responsibility to be swift to hear and slow to speak?

PRAYER

Adonai my God, in my unrighteous indignation, I have only had ears for me. Forgive me, Father, for the deafness of my heart, and teach me to listen past my rage with unstopped ears and a shut-up mouth. As I grow "swift to hear" and "slow to speak," help me to understand the words of others unfiltered by my own emotions and enmity—unfounded or otherwise. Show me, God, how to find peace during intense disagreement, that in opening my ears and closing my mouth, I will finally find Your righteousness.

Chapter 7

Receive the Word, Then Do It!

> Therefore, having put aside all filthiness and superabundance of evil, in humility be receiving the ingrafted word that is able to save your souls, and become doers of the word, and not hearers only, *thereby* deceiving yourselves. Because if anyone is a hearer of the word and not a doer, this one has been likened to a man viewing his natural face in a mirror, for he viewed himself, and went away, and immediately forgot what kind of *man* he was. But he who looked into the perfect תּוֹרָה, Torah—that of liberty—and continued there, *was* not a forgetful hearer, but a doer of action. This one will be happy in his doing.
>
> יַעֲקֹב YA'AQOV 1:21-25 (MJLT)

THE WORD OF TRUTH—that sweet, sweet, powerful sound—lies dormant and useless before us. We sit. And listen. And hear. We revel in the sound it makes, and it stirs us up... inside. Though we invite it in and absorb its perfection, it ultimately does nothing but serve as fodder for our minds' feeble and fruitless activities. The word is rendered wholly weak and inert... unless and until the time we begin to put the word *into action*.

With the best of intentions and the humility of hope, many of us start our walk toward obedience by making room for the word in our lives. At great displeasure to our selves, we "put aside all filthiness and superabundance of evil"—turning our backs on sin and the ongoing corruption of our souls—and in its place, receive the word. But then, the ingrafting having taken hold, too many of us mistakenly believe that the work is over. Sadly, the saving word, now firmly set in place where it may begin its eternal work, remains unactivated.

This is the great deception that we perpetrate upon ourselves: simply *receive* the word—*accept* the Messiah—and you will be changed. But this oversimplified thinking reveals the false expectation that passive belief in or acceptance of God will result in a dynamic transformation of our lives. No wonder so many who name Yeshua as Messiah walk away before any change has a chance to take place. We have failed to realize that the word of truth demands not a *passive* but an *active response*—that is, we must "become doers of the word, and not hearers only."

When many of us hear the word, it generally makes sense to us—it rings true, offers us hope, gives us direction, inspires us, brings us comfort, dictates our values, informs our beliefs, and marks the boundaries for our acceptable, godly behavior. But unless the hearing is followed instantly by the doing, then what we have heard will just as quickly be forgotten. It is as futile, ridiculous and sad as "a man viewing his natural face in a mirror, [who] went away, and immediately forgot what kind of *man* he was." We do not stare into a mirror merely to view our own enchanting reflection, but rather to see ourselves as we are *in reality* reflected to the world. How useless does that mirror become if what we see does not show us who we are?

But the mirror that is the word teaches us that we do not normally see ourselves as we truly are. Our self-perception is naturally *and mistakenly* formed by how we view ourselves *apart* from the word. But when we look intently into the word *and continue there*, it sets us free to see not only the truest reflection of ourselves, but how we presently reflect the truth of God. It is through this mirror that we may peer most deeply into ourselves, and as long as we do not walk away, we will never forget what it shows us, but will instead be compelled to act upon it.

As a "doer of action," every disciple of Messiah must move beyond the passivity of a *believer* into the activity of a *follower*. To activate the word of God in our lives, yes, we begin with inspiration, devotion, meditation and study; but then, we must transcend and move beyond the feeding of our hearts and minds, and enact the word with our hands, feet and tongues. To be our true selves, we must actively apply the word not just in our thinking, but by the transformation of those thoughts into obedience to the word. For indeed, "this one will be happy in his doing."

QUESTIONS

Chapter 7

1. Even after we have "put aside all filthiness and superabundance of evil," there is more to be done. What is required on our part in order for the word to do its work of saving our souls? Why is it not enough to passively receive the word, and then simply wait for our lives to be transformed?

2. Ya'aqov exhorts us to be "doers of the word, and not hearers only." Explain the difference between being a hearer and a doer of the word. How does hearing the word without putting it into action cause you to deceive yourself?

3. One who "is a hearer of the word and not a doer" is like someone who walks away from a mirror and forgets his own image. When we continually look into the word as into a mirror, what

does it teach us about ourselves? How does failing to enact the word cause us to forget who we are?

4. It is not enough to just be believers; we must be followers as well. In what specific areas do you need to take the word that you believe in your heart and mind, and put it into action with your hands, feet and tongue? What are the first steps you are going to take?

---------- PRAYER ----------

Master Yeshua, Your word is life… now please help me to find the conviction to live it. Let me not be satisfied with only an inward belief, ADONAI, but cause me to activate and live my faith both boldly and outwardly. Wake me up, Father, so that I am no longer just a passive believer, but an active follower of Your truth. I receive Your word, O God; enact it powerfully in me, that I may accurately reflect the reality of Your Son.

Chapter 8

Devotion Pure and Undefiled

> If anyone thinks *himself* to be devout—not bridling his tongue, but *rather* deceiving his heart—the devotion of this one *is* vain. Devotion pure and undefiled with the God and Father is this: to look after orphans and widows in their oppression, *and* to keep himself unspotted from the world.
>
> יַעֲקֹב *YA'AQOV 1:26-27 (MJLT)*

IF YOU WERE TRULY DEVOTED TO GOD—if you were devout—how would you conduct yourself? What does that even look like? Would you spend an hour each morning at dawn reading your Bible, praying, listening to uplifting music, and sipping a latte? Would you act more religiously—regularly attending worship services, reciting the prayers or affirmations, and embracing the rituals, trappings and calendar of the established traditions?

But what if devotion is deeper than that? Simpler? What if true devotion has nothing to do with religion or "devotions" at all, but is instead about being consumed with God in every single thought, word and action?

"If anyone thinks *himself* to be devout," he may want to think again. Devotion is not something that God simply credits to our account just because we have reduced our walk with Him to manageable, repetitive religious habit. Rather, by nature, it is supposed to be dynamic, spontaneous and responsive in any given situation. Devotion is the intersection between our daily life and the degree to which we welcome God to rule it. It is an accurate reflection of how we are *really* relating to Yeshua—right now.

For example, when everything we have to say is negative and critical and prideful, or we speak out harshly in anger or frustration, or we simply run off at the mouth—saying whatever unfiltered thought that pops into our head—we are "not bridling [our] tongue, but *rather* deceiving [our] heart," demonstrating without doubt how truly undevoted we are to God. Instead, this shows how dedicated we are to ourselves—our own mind and thoughts—and how devoid our spirit is of divine and Scriptural influence.

So whether we are deficient in our words and attitudes toward others, or we speak and act insensitively or selfishly in our relationships, or we automatically follow our fleshly instincts whenever we feel desire, or we give in to our emotions rather than seeking the mind of God, or we ignore or fail to consult the Scriptures when faced with choices and decisions, or we neglect to proclaim the Messiah in our everyday encounters—especially when our daily interaction with Him is rote and vague and trivial and lifeless—"the devotion of this one *is* vain."

When God is not sufficiently invited into our normal, ordinary daily lives—and we are not sufficiently engaged with Him in it—no amount of compartmentalized prayer, Bible study, praise, worship, congregational attendance, tradition or ritual will amount to "devotion pure and undefiled" in the eyes of God. Instead, it is "vain," empty, useless and worthless. It is devoid of anything that would connect us to God and the world around us in a significantly meaningful way.

Instead, "devotion pure and undefiled with the God and Father is this: to look after orphans and widows in their oppression, *and* to keep himself unspotted from the world." A defiled, impure devotion is self-pleasing and introverted, pursuing God with self-serving motives, or in obliviousness toward outside causes and needs. But an undefiled, pure devotion is set on pleasing God and meeting the needs of others. It is extroverted—it serves and runs after God with self-sacrificial motives, consciously aware of both the need to act outwardly on behalf of others, as well as the necessity to act inwardly in pursuit of purity and sinlessness.

It's time to evaluate and reflect upon the quality and kind of our devotion. Does it reveal that we have relegated God to one religious corner of our lives? Or does it reflect the self-sacrificial walk of a slave whose life is consumed with the will of his Master? Don't deceive your heart any longer; today, make your devotion pure and undefiled.

QUESTIONS

Chapter 8

1. As followers of Yeshua, we all want to believe that we are wholly devoted to God. Why do we often use our participation in spiritual activities or religious events as a measure of our level of devotion? How do these things fail to give an accurate reflection of how devout we truly are?

2. When we think we are devout but don't control our tongues, we deceive ourselves. What kinds of things might be spoken by a person with an unbridled tongue? If you evaluated your own devoutness by all the words you spoke this past week, what would you conclude?

3. If devotion is about being consumed with God in every single thought, word and action, then we all have room to grow.

In what areas do you need to more fully invite God into your normal, ordinary daily life? What changes do you think will happen as a result?

4. According to Ya'aqov, pure and undefiled devotion is "to look after orphans and widows in their oppression, *and* to keep [one]self unspotted from the world." How does meeting the needs of others demonstrate our devotion to God? What does it mean to be unspotted from the world?

PRAYER

God and Father of Heaven and earth, give me a simple and singular devotion toward You. Cure me, Master, of my vain and repetitive religion that I routinely mistake for dedication and love. I invite You, ADONAI, into my normal, everyday life—I welcome You to rule every moment of it completely. May my responsiveness to You, God, be unrehearsed and undefiled; may my devotion reflect a heart that is ever pleasing and pure.

Chapter 9

Bringing the King's Torah to Its Goal

My brothers, do not hold the faith of the glory of our Master יֵשׁוּעַ, Yeshua *the* Messiah in favoritism. For if there comes into your synagogue a man with a gold ring, *dressed* in bright clothing, and there also comes in a poor man in shabby clothing, and you look upon him wearing the bright clothing and say, "You—sit here well-*situated*," and to the poor man say, "You—stand there," or "Sit under my footstool," did you not make distinctions fully among yourselves, and *so* become ill-reasoning judges? Listen, my beloved brothers: did not God choose the poor in the world *to be* rich in faith, and heirs of the Reign that He promised to those loving Him?... If, indeed, you bring *the* King's תּוֹרָה, Torah to its goal according to the Scripture, "You must love your neighbor as yourself," you do well; but if you show favoritism, you enact sin, *and are* being convicted by the תּוֹרָה, Torah as sidesteppers.

יַעֲקֹב *YA'AQOV 2:1-9 (MJLT)*

My favorite ice cream is peanut butter and chocolate—hands down. Sure, a scoop of top-quality sea salt caramel gelato is *unbelievable*, but if you put the two in front of me and forced me to choose ("What? I can't have *both?*"), I would pick the peanut butter and chocolate all day, every day. Why? I don't know. It's yummy. That's the one I like. It's my favorite.

We all choose favorites at one time or another. We have favorite foods, colors, clothes, books, songs, sports teams, movies, weather, pets, you name it. Sometimes—probably more often than we should—we even have favorite people: people we like to be with and do things for and, frankly, show preferential treatment. While it's one thing to show *favor* to someone, especially in times of need, it's quite another to show *favoritism* based merely on the other person's station in life, or how they look, or our feelings toward them, or our own personal biases and preferences.

When dealing with people—especially people we are biased against—we disciples of Messiah are not allowed to show favoritism... ever. The way we demonstrate our faith and put it into action—the way we live out who we are in Messiah—is to act the same way toward all people, regardless of who they are, or how much (or how little) we like them. We cannot elevate or denigrate people because they do not fit in our social or political class, or they dress poorly, or they smell funny, or they don't like chocolate and peanut butter (what kind of person doesn't like chocolate and peanut butter?!). When the distinctions we make between people lead us to showing some people favoritism over others, we become "ill-reasoning judges," unworthy of the faith we represent and the resources with which we have been entrusted.

In God's big, beautiful irony, "did not [He] choose the poor in the world *to be* rich in faith, and heirs of the Reign that He promised to those loving Him?" While our superficial, small minds want to be partial to people who are financially successful, particularly well-dressed, good-looking, smart, clever, or even those who just share our worldly values and ideals, God cares nothing for these things where the exercise of our faith is concerned. Rather, He gives abundantly to those we might otherwise deem unfit, so long as they love Him richly.

As Messiah-followers, we are not entitled to "hold the faith of the glory of our Master יֵשׁוּעַ, Yeshua *the* Messiah in favoritism." On the contrary, our job as His disciples is to "bring *the* King's תּוֹרָה, Torah to its goal according to the Scripture, 'You must love your neighbor as yourself.'" By not passing judgment or withholding love, we reflect God's love, and in this we "do well." "[B]ut if you show favoritism, you enact sin, *and are* being convicted by the תּוֹרָה, Torah as sidesteppers." Favoritism misses the goal.

The temptation to show favoritism is great, especially because it disguises itself as the desire to be nice to some—while, in reality, demanding the mistreatment of others. Know your biases and resist them. Bring God's Torah to its goal by showing the same love to all.

QUESTIONS

Chapter 9

1. To illustrate favoritism, Ya'aqov uses the example of giving the best seat to a rich man, while giving the worst seat—or no seat at all—to a poor man. What are some modern examples of ways we might show favoritism based on a person's social status or our own biases? Why is favoritism sinful?

2. When we show favoritism, we "become ill-reasoning judges." Explain how judgments based on superficial characteristics or personal preferences show our lack of good reasoning. How is this type of judgment different from the type of judgment instructed by Paul in 1 Corinthians 5:11-6:3?

3. God turns the world's values and ideals upside down, choosing "the poor in the world *to be* rich in faith." Besides wealth, what are some attributes that society greatly values, but God sees as meaningless? How have you allowed society's distinc-

tions and judgments to affect the value you place on other people?

4. By showing favoritism, we violate the command to love our neighbors as ourselves, and are guilty of sin. Why is it difficult to show love to those who are different from us, or those with whom we disagree? How can we overcome those biases, and show the same love to all?

PRAYER

I confess, Father, I have been infected with favoritism—I have allowed my personal biases toward those who don't share my values to affect the way I treat them outwardly, and the compassion I should have for them in my heart. Teach me, Master, to stop making distinctions between people as far as sharing or withholding Your love is concerned. Help me, ADONAI, to neither elevate nor denigrate others, but to act the same way toward all, regardless of how they treat me. Let me not miss the goal of Your Torah, O God, but always equally dispense Your unbiased love.

Chapter 10

The Torah of Liberty— So Speak, and So Do

For whoever keeps the whole תּוֹרָה, Torah, and stumbles in one POINT, has become guilty of *breaking it* all. For He who is saying, "YOU MUST NOT COMMIT ADULTERY," also said, "YOU MUST NOT MURDER." And *so*, if you do not commit adultery, yet *you* commit murder, you have become a sidestepper of תּוֹרָה, Torah. *Therefore*, as *ones who are* about to be judged by a תּוֹרָה, Torah of liberty, so speak, and so do; for the judgment without *loving*-kindness *IS shown* to him *who* has not done *loving*-kindness *to others*; *loving*-kindness triumphs over judgment.

יַעֲקֹב *YA'AQOV 2:10-13 (MJLT)*

EVERYONE—EVERYWHERE—YEARNS TO BE FREE. Strangely, the definition of freedom changes from one person to the next, and what you may perceive as boundless freedom might be a dungeon-like prison to me. But regardless of the type of thing we each call freedom, no one disagrees that in order to be truly free we must be free of anyone telling us what we should think, what we can say, or what we can do... no one disagrees, that is, except for the true disciple of Messiah.

For many believers, their reaction to the idea that "whoever keeps the whole תּוֹרָה, Torah, and stumbles in one point, has become guilty of breaking it all," is to say, "See! We don't need to keep all those rules! It would be unjust for God to tell us we have to do all those things, and then to find us guilty when we can't. And God is not unjust!" But this is not the point at all. The reality is that unless we are completely ungoverned by any set of values or beliefs or morals—in other words, rules—then we are cherry-picking according to our own individual sense of "freedom." This is why "if you do not commit adultery, yet you commit murder, you have become a sidestepper of תּוֹרָה, Torah." The point is not whether one is capable of keeping the Torah perfectly, and thus avoiding guilt, but rather that the rules are there for a reason, and one does not have the "freedom" to keep some and dismiss the others.

Such thinking reveals a wrong-headed approach to freedom. Freedom is not anarchy—the eschewing of rules, the absence of law and order. Freedom is not the unleashing of base desires, or the license to act upon impulse with no limits or boundaries. On the contrary, in order for freedom to exist—in order for it to function—we need to be able to distinguish bad from good, wrong from right, dangerous from safe. We need to know where it's okay to go, and where it's not. That's the purpose of the rules.

And yet, while many of us accept the necessity of the rules and say we are willing to abide by them, the idea that we can be free while at the same time having what we think, say, and do dictated to us is unimaginable. Of course, we have to live within the boundaries of certain thick, black lines, but placing restrictions on every single thing that comes out of our mouths and is done with our hands? Surely, that's not freedom in any sense of the word!

What we need to realize, however, is that the same Torah that provides the rules—that says where it's okay to go, and draws those thick, black lines—is the same Torah that also sets people free; it is "a תּוֹרָה, Torah of liberty." And because that Torah liberates those *"who are* about to be judged by" it, for them, there is but a single unavoidable directive: "so speak, and so do."

The way we love our neighbors—the way we treat each other, the way we display or withhold loving-kindness—is all wrapped up in everything we say and do. We find liberty, then, by adhering to the dictates of Scripture, not because it is confining and restricting (though it certainly is), but because it limits the extent to which we can hate, and treat each other poorly, and live in all manner of sin. The liberty provided by the Word releases us from the weighty burden that comes from choosing to color outside the lines.

If we are truly Messiah's disciples, we are *not* free to think and speak and do as we please. Rather, we must live according to the Scriptures, because by the loving-kindness it teaches we will be judged. Will we act according to our own ideas of liberty? Or will we let the word of God constrain us to what we may do? This is the true freedom.

QUESTIONS

Chapter 10

1. Although we all yearn to be free, our definitions of freedom are not always the same. Explain the difference between a freedom that has no limits or boundaries, and the freedom we have in Messiah. How is it possible for the same rules that put boundaries on our behavior to also give us freedom?

2. Ya'aqov says that we are *"ones who are about to be judged by a* תּוֹרָה*, Torah of liberty."* Does that then give us the freedom to pick and choose which rules we will keep and which we will dismiss? Why, or why not? What does the Torah of liberty protect us from?

3. Why are we generally willing to submit to certain broad rules (e.g., do not murder), but recoil at the idea of restrictions on every single thing we say or do? What are some of the limits

Scripture places on our words and our actions, especially regarding our interactions with others?

4. We usually don't have difficulty showing loving-kindness to those we feel deserve it, but what about those we view as unworthy? Why is it necessary to show loving-kindness (mercy) to them as well? If you were to be judged according to the same loving-kindness you show to others, what would be the result?

--- PRAYER ---

ADONAI, my God, constrain and restrict me—cast off the shackles of my own sense of freedom. Show me, Father, Your just and perfect judgment, that I may embrace the freeing and righteous limitations of Your word. Teach me, Master, to not speak and do how I please, but to restrain my words and actions to Your truth. I praise Your Name, Father, and Your protective ways of liberty, for in You alone am I truly and forever set free.

Chapter 11

Not By Faith Only

What *is* the profit, my brothers, if anyone speaks of having faith, but he does not have actions? Is that faith able to save him?... [T]he faith by itself, if it does not have actions, is dead. But someone might say, "You have faith, and I have actions." Show me your faith apart from the actions, and I will show you by my actions, the faith!... [B]y actions is man declared righteous, and not by faith only.... For *just* as the body apart from the רוּחַ, ruach is dead, so also the faith apart from actions is dead!

יַעֲקֹב YA'AQOV 2:14-26 (MJLT)

WE SIT AND LISTEN; WE STUDY AND READ. We pray. We praise. We seek. We believe. How, then, could it be possible that our faith might actually be *dead?* How, with all our prayers, all our devotion, all our focus on the things of God, all our time spent in His word, could the ability of our faith to save us be honestly doubted? Surely, we are doing all that God expects of us. Unquestionably, He merely desires that we believe. What could we possibly be missing?

When we say that we have faith in the Messiah Yeshua, what we are actually declaring—though we may not realize it—is that we are unable to resist emulating the One in whom we believe... that our beliefs are self-compelled to externalize and manifest themselves through action. We betray that faith, then, when we reduce it to thoughts and feelings, and suppress the actions that our faith should naturally produce. "What *is* the profit" of such a faith? What good is it to anyone?

What good is it, for example, to see a brother or sister in need, and say, "I'll pray for you!" but not give them what they need? What good is it to meet people who need to be saved, but only say to them, "God bless you!" and not tell them of the salvation they are missing? "What *is* the profit *to that person's life?* So also, the faith by itself, if it does not have actions, is dead" (vs.16-17).

Is there not something living and burning inside of us? Has not God awoken our spirit, shown us mysteries, and given us purpose? But if our faith is dormant—dead inside us—then an actionless faith faithfully represents the kind of faith we truly have. Or perhaps that faith is still breathing, yet it does not have actions because we are actively suffocating it—snuffing it out—by our passivity, fear, and lack of compassion and care. We smother and kill our own faith by keeping it from taking action.

"But someone might say, 'You have faith, and I have actions,'" which clearly misses the point. To suppose that faith can exist without actions, or actions without faith, is to grant them each a power that neither one has on its own. A good or charitable action not produced by faith may bring help in time of need, but it is ultimately meaningless. An inward, actionless faith that "believe[s] that God is One" indicates belief, but it is essentially pointless—"*even* the demons believe *that*, and they shudder *at the thought*" (v. 19). True actions will always flow from faith. True faith will always result in action. "Show me your faith apart from the actions, and I will show you by my actions, the faith!"

So then, no matter what good, holy, or upright thing we think, feel, say, or believe, "faith apart from... actions is [both dead and] inactive" (v. 20), since it is "by actions [that] man [is] declared righteous, and not by faith only." Take Av'raham, for example, whose belief was credited to him as righteousness *because he put his faith into action* when he brought Yitz'chaq up to the sacrificial altar (see בְּרֵאשִׁית B'reshiyt 22). "Do you see that the faith was working with his actions, and by the actions the faith was perfected" (v. 22)? If we merely *believe* we are righteous, yet do not *do* righteousness through our actions, such a faith is inactive, imperfect, and, quite possibly, unrighteous.

Like a body without its spirit is dead, "so also the faith apart from actions is dead!" If our faith is real—if it is true, if it is alive—then we must imitate our Master and *activate it.* Where there is a need, we fill it. Where there is a soul, we reach out to it. We focus not on ourselves, but on the needs of others; we sacrifice for righteousness' sake, and seek not our own benefit. How full or empty is your faith today? Make sure it's alive and "able to save."

QUESTIONS

Chapter 11

1. Ya'aqov speaks of faith that is dead and unable to save. Explain how it is possible to spend time in God's word, in praise and prayer, and in fellowship with other believers, and yet still have a faith that is dead. If we reduce our faith to spiritual thoughts and feelings, how is that faith able to benefit anyone?

2. For some of us, our faith lacks action because we are actively suffocating it. List some attitudes and behaviors that keep us from putting our faith into action. What happens when we suppress the actions that our faith should naturally produce?

3. When we try to separate actions and faith, we miss the point. Why are good actions produced without faith ultimately as

meaningless as an inward, actionless faith? How does Av'-raham's righteousness illustrate the proper relationship between faith and actions?

4. Now is the time to evaluate your faith and make sure it is alive and active. In what ways are you doing well at putting your faith into action, and in what ways are you falling short? What changes do you need to make in order to more fully activate your faith?

PRAYER

ADONAI my God, reveal to my heart the true state of my faith, whether it is alert and alive, or barely breathing. Show me, Master, if my belief is rightly reflecting Your ways, and help me to take action wherever it is not. Revive my spirit, Father—spark me to life—that my faith and focus may not be sickly, dormant or dead. Stir up my soul, Yeshua; shake me loose of my passiveness and apathy. Resuscitate my faith and make it able to save.

Chapter 12

For We All Make Many Stumbles

> Many *of you should* not become teachers, my brothers —having known that we *who teach* will receive greater judgment—for we all make many stumbles.
>
> יַעֲקֹב YA'AQOV 3:1-2A (MJLT)

IT CAN BE AN EXHILARATING EXPERIENCE to see something new in the Scriptures—to be reading through or studying a familiar passage, and then suddenly have the words leap off the page and grab our attention, as if for the first time. It is a stirring reminder that the word of God is alive—that the Scriptures are a thoroughly spiritual document—and that through it, God is actively speaking to us, engaging us, and interacting with our daily lives.

But sometimes, some of us will make a dire mistake.

When we see that new thing, instead of simply being thrilled at finding something we had totally missed before, we literally start to see it as a completely "new" thing... something *no one* has seen before. As it unspools within our creative mind, this newly revealed "hidden truth" distorts, and warps, and becomes a filter for us—a key—by which all Scripture can now be "truly" discerned.

Some of us, then, will take to the internet—or our study groups, or congregations—to spread our new discovery...

...and others of us will gleefully repeat it.

It's an alarming phenomenon, for sure—and, unfortunately, one that is all too prevalent among Messianic, "Jewish roots," and "Hebraic roots" believers. Since the prevailing approach in such circles is already to go against the grain of traditional Christianity, this naturally fosters a susceptibility to debatable ideas. Indeed, it can be quite exciting, and often a relief, to discover that there are biblical answers to the myriad of unbiblical Christian doctrines and practices. But in our zeal over newfound truths, some of us turn our backs on "old" truths—even real truth embedded at the core of Christianity—and ironically open ourselves up to new kinds of *errors* (or new versions of old ones). In realizing that there is truth beyond the four walls of the church, we become willing to entertain any "new" idea we can get our hands on.

This is very much like the attitude of the Athenians Paul was addressing in Acts 17:21, who "were spending their time on nothing else but to say something *novel*, or to hear some newer thing." In what hopefully began as a legitimate search for the truth, some of us have instead overreached; we stopped accepting the plain teachings of Scripture in lieu of more "novel" ideas allegedly still *based* in Scripture. For too many of us, the simple word of God no longer satisfies, as we have developed stranger appetites. In the unending quest for answers, we have ended up calling our entire faith into question.

To be clear, there is nothing wrong with questioning what we have been taught—and, oftentimes, even questioning those who taught us. What is wrong is being reckless with the Scriptures, unintentionally or not, and allowing our own clever ideas and imaginations to impose themselves on God's word.

It's time to reevaluate the unorthodox teachings—and teachers—we are listening to. When we hear of new theologies or new ways of looking at Scripture, we need to be wary, not excited. We should be slow to embrace unconventional teachings, no matter how much sense they make to our hearts and minds. We also need to consider the source of such teachings and the ramifications they have on long-held beliefs: does the teaching truly right an interpretive wrong, or does it serve an underlying agenda? We should beware of doctrines that cause division or confusion. We must be careful of theologies that foster militant or negative attitudes. We need to be on guard against teachings that challenge the plain, logical sense of Scripture.

The warning of greater judgment to would-be teachers is a warning to us all, since we don't have to be "teachers" in order to propagate bad teachings. Let us be mindful, then, of our tendency to believe a good-sounding idea over good, sound teaching—"for we all make many stumbles."

QUESTIONS

Chapter 12

1. Can you remember a time when you discovered something in the Scriptures that you had never seen before? If so, describe how it made you feel. When someone distorts a "hidden truth," making it into a key for "truly" understanding all Scripture, how does that idea so easily get passed on to others?

2. Many people begin searching for answers because they see errors in Christianity, only to end up straying from the truth. How can a legitimate search for truth be turned into something that is dangerous to our faith? Why do you think the discovery of "new" ideas is so appealing for some of us?

3. Rather than eagerly embracing every new teaching we hear, we should always be cautious. What are some warning signs

that a particular teaching might be incorrect, and perhaps even dangerous? How can you distinguish between a teaching that sounds biblical, and a teaching that is biblically sound?

4. Ya'aqov warns that many of us should not become teachers, "for we all make many stumbles." How should you evaluate those whose teachings you consume, in order to determine if they are trustworthy? Why do you need to be careful about which teachings you pass along to others?

--- PRAYER ---

Master Yeshua, in my zeal for You, I may have been undiscerning concerning Your word. I can sometimes be too easily enamored with my own ideas, or too trusting with the ideas of others. Help me, Father, to not simply accept everything I'm told, and to not seek the novelty of new winds of teaching. Enlighten my mind, ADONAI, to the unchanging truth of Your word, that I may not stumble and fall upon the presumptions of mine.

Chapter 13

The Tongue: World of the Unrighteousness

> If anyone does not stumble in word, this one *is* a perfect man, able to also bridle the whole body. Now if we put the bits into the mouths of the horses for their being persuaded by us, *then* we *can* also turn about their whole body. Look! also the ships *of the sea*—being so great, and being driven by fierce winds—are led about by a very small rudder, wherever the impulse of the helmsman wants. So also the tongue is a little member *of the body*, yet *it* boasts greatly. Look! such a little fire—*yet* how great a forest it sets aflame! And *so* the tongue *is* a fire—the world of the unrighteousness.
>
> יעקב YA'AQOV 3:2B-6A (MJLT)

THE ABILITY TO SPEAK—the capacity to formulate thoughts in our minds, and then to express those thoughts vocally in a way that other people can understand—is a miraculous gift from God to man. One would think that the mouth and the tongue are necessarily subservient to the mind, such that one is only capable of saying what he is thinking. But many times—too many times—it seems as if our tongue has a mind of its own. We speak "without thinking," and then claim we didn't mean what we said. Or we say *exactly* what we're thinking, although we didn't intend to say it out loud. How is such a phenomenon possible? Can our tongues actually speak independently of our minds?

The Scriptures draw several comparisons to illustrate the tongue's uncanny—and seemingly autonomous—ability. First, the tongue is likened to a tiny bit in a horse's mouth, able to persuade the large animal to turn its whole body to either side. It is also compared to the "very small rudder" of a ship, which—despite the driving, fierce winds—still leads the vessel "wherever the impulse of the helmsman wants" it to go. And, finally, the Scriptures say that the tongue is "such a little fire," yet, when left unattended and unchecked, it has the potential to set an entire forest ablaze.

For such a "little member *of the body*," the tongue certainly "boasts greatly"—and with good reason. Indeed, the tongue is exceptionally mighty, and wields powerful control over the whole entity to which it belongs. Like the horse's bit and the ship's rudder, the tongue can make us go where it wants, leading us into fights or conflict or regret from speaking things we should not have said. And like the little fire that grows to engulf the forest in flames, the tongue can rage out of control. Speaking out of a place of hurt or anger—or even zeal—it can raze its listeners to the ground.

"And *so* the tongue *is* a fire—the world of the unrighteousness." When we let our tongues speak every thought in any circumstance—giving no heed to our state of mind, caring nothing for the one to whom we are speaking, and having no concern for the consequences of our words—we unleash an inferno of unrighteousness upon the earth. Truth and lie alike become agents of manipulation, interchanged in our mouth as they serve the tongue's unrighteous ends. Permitted to run amok, the unstoppable flow from our lips spews forth, leaving us only to follow in the path of our own tongue's destructive devastation.

So the tongue, then, indeed, is a horse's bit—but it still needs a rider to pull it. The tongue is the rudder of a stalwart ship—but it still needs a helmsman to steer it. The tongue is a fire that consumes the timberland—but it still needs the spark to ignite it. We are the rider, the helmsman, and the spark: no, the tongue does not have a mind of its own; we supply all the unrighteousness it needs.

To ascribe power to the tongue is simply to acknowledge that we are in control of and responsible for everything we say. When we speak "without thinking" or say things we didn't "mean," it's not our tongue doing the talking, but our inner secrets and deepest emotions, as we let loose the reins of self-control and allow our minds to run wild without restraint. "If anyone does not stumble in word, this one *is* a perfect man, able to also bridle the whole body." Know the power of your words, and the unrighteousness they can bring. Then bridle yourself by controlling your tongue, and "stumble in word" no more.

QUESTIONS
───────────

Chapter 13

1. At one time or another, we have all said things that we came to regret. How is it possible for us to say things that we later claim we didn't really mean, or to speak thoughts that we didn't intend to say out loud? Why do you think it is so easy to speak "without thinking"?

2. In what ways can the tongue steer the course of our lives (like a bit or rudder) or bring about destruction (like a fire)? Describe a time when you personally experienced the tongue's devastating power, either through words someone spoke to you, or words you spoke to someone else.

3. Ya'aqov calls the tongue "the world of the unrighteousness." Is it possible to be a righteous person, and yet have a tongue that spews unrighteousness? Why, or why not? Explain how

even words of zealousness or truth can be used in an unrighteous manner.

4. If you were to honestly examine all of your words—from comments typed to strangers on the internet, to conversations with your closest loved ones—what would you discover about yourself? What steps do you need to take in order to more fully bridle yourself by controlling your tongue?

PRAYER

ADONAI, my Creator, You spoke me into existence; forgive me for not speaking life into others in return. Teach me, Master, to not simply hold my tongue, but to bridle my entire body and mind with Your holiness. Help me, Father, to think before I speak, and to realize that everything I say is a true reflection of my heart. Give me Your mind, Yeshua, so that Your pure word may flow from my lips, and my tongue may be used only to glorify Your righteousness.

Chapter 14

The Tongue's Deadly Poison

In this manner, the tongue is set in our *body's* members *as that* which is polluting our whole body, and is setting on fire the course of *our fleshly* nature, and is *itself* set on fire by the גֵּיהִנֹּם, Geihinom. For every *kind of animal in* nature... is subdued, and has been subdued, by the human's nature. But the tongue, no one of men is able to subdue. *It is* an uncontrollable evil, full of deadly poison. With it we bless the Master and Father, and with it we curse the men *who have been* made according to the likeness of God; out of the same mouth comes forth blessing and cursing—it is not necessary, my brothers, *for* these things to happen this way! Does the fountain—out of the same opening—pour out *both* the sweet and the bitter *water*? Is a fig-tree able, my brothers, to make olives? or a vine, figs? Nor *can* salt water make fresh.

יַעֲקֹב *YA'AQOV 3:6B-12 (MJLT)*

THE TONGUE—THAT SMALL, YET POWERFUL INSTIGATOR—SEEKS to wield control over our whole being. It finds its fuel in our innermost thoughts and emotions, and then overwhelms our self-control, unleashing its unrighteous destruction upon others. Nevertheless, the tongue has no authority of its own. It is only able to do according to that which we allow and provide. And yet, we supply the tongue not only its power, but also the means to spread its poison.

Of all our body's members that may be used to devastate and destroy, the tongue rises above the rest. Its venom is able to pollute our whole body, breathing life into the most contemptible of thoughts and ideas. Once spoken aloud, the unspoken becomes real, and we give ourselves over to its sway. Let loose on a rampage, the tongue sets our whole flesh on fire, and our remaining members willingly follow it into the blaze.

When we allow the tongue to take control, we are channeling the very fires of Hell itself. The essence of the place reserved for eternal torment and punishment of the ungodly is vomited from our mouths, spraying like an acid upon any object of our unholy wrath. The foe standing before us (that person we may have even loved a moment earlier) becomes saturated by the fury of unending fire. It is an unmerciful force that we ourselves summoned and invited to spew forth from our lips.

Once birthed by fire and brought to life, the malevolent, vengeful, lying tongue is utterly unstoppable. Though human beings are able to overcome many an obstacle and overpower many an enemy, where the tongue is concerned, "no one of men is able to subdue" it. The tongue's hellish source surges through it, making it "an uncontrollable evil" that lashes, whips and cuts deeply. In each wound it leaves behind a "deadly poison" that worms like a disease through its victim—it ravages and guts him from the inside out long after the encounter has ended.

And yet, the vilest of the tongue's activities springs from its hypocrisy. This tongue of power and poison, with which "we curse the men *who have been* made according to the likeness of God," is the same tongue with which we abundantly and magnificently "bless the Master and Father." Indeed, "out of the same mouth comes forth blessing and cursing"—which ought to be a literal impossibility for a disciple of Messiah. This is, of course, not only evil, but a perversion of our new nature in Him. "Does the fountain—out of the same opening—pour out *both* the sweet and the bitter *water?* Is a fig-tree able, my brothers, to make olives? or a vine, figs? Nor *can* salt water make fresh." For blessing and cursing to come from the same tongue is an abomination to God and His new creation.

Thankfully, "it is not necessary, my brothers, *for* these things to happen this way!"—we have the antidote for the poison. If we are truly in Yeshua, then we must unfork our tongue and douse its hell-fire with the waters of blessing. We must recant all the evil we have spoken, and apply the healing balm of remorse through apology. Reassert control over yourself, and permit your tongue only the power to speak life—pour out the sweet blessings of Yeshua, and curse others in bitterness no more.

QUESTIONS

Chapter 14

1. Ya'aqov says that our tongue is "polluting our whole body, and is setting on fire the course of *our fleshly* nature." Explain how the tongue is able to influence the other members of our bodies. When you speak sinful thoughts and ideas aloud, what effects does it have?

2. What does Ya'aqov mean when he says that the tongue is "set on fire by the גֵּיהִנֹּם, Geihinom [Hell]" and is "full of deadly poison"? If you think back to times when you spoke destructive words, how does it make you feel to know that what came out of your mouth was truly evil?

3. When we use our mouth both to bless God and to curse men, we are perverting the new nature we have been given. What types of words do we use that are actually a curse against

those made in "the likeness of God"? In what way are such words incompatible with using our mouths to bless God?

4. According to Ya'aqov, "it is not necessary... *for* these things to happen this way." Since "no one of men is able to subdue" the tongue, how is it possible for you to stop allowing evil words to come out of your mouth? If there are people you have hurt with your words, what actions should you take right now?

PRAYER

O Father, my tongue has let loose an unholy fire and deadly poison from Hell; forgive me for willfully spewing my rage, hate and insecurity. Heal those I have hurt, Yeshua, and counteract the venom I have injected into my victims. Change my heart, ADONAI, and fill my mouth and mind with words of remorse and restoration. Even in my hurt and anger, Master, please subdue my poisonous tongue. Teach me to not speak in bitter curses, but to pour out a sweet fountain of blessing.

Chapter 15

Who Among You Is Wise and Understanding?

Who *is* wise and understanding among you? Let him show *it* by the good behavior—his actions in humility of wisdom. But if you have bitter jealousy and *selfish* ambition in your heart, boast not, nor lie against the truth: this "wisdom" is not descending from above, but *is* earthly, physical, demon-like. For where jealousy and *selfish* ambition ARE, there is disorder and every evil practice. But the wisdom from above, first, indeed, is pure, then peaceable, gentle, cooperative, full of *loving*-kindness and good fruits, uncontentious, and unhypocritical; and the fruit of righteousness in peace is sown to those making peace.

יַעֲקֹב *YA'AQOV 3:13-18 (MJLT)*

WHO, INDEED, IS WISE? For many of us, wisdom is only for the learned, the scholarly, those well-versed in the knowledge of the ages. For others, wisdom is for the experienced, the aged, those who have learned from the hard teachings of a long life. For others still, having wisdom is knowing the difference between right and wrong, and possessing the judgment or discernment to offer insight and guidance to others. But what if true wisdom and understanding are not simply based on how much we know—and on the nature of those things we know—but on where that wisdom comes from, and how it is put into use? What if what we think of as wisdom is not really wisdom at all?

The evidence that we are wise is not necessarily proven by what or how much we know. On the contrary, according to the Scriptures, wisdom is shown by our "good behavior—[by] actions in humility of wisdom." In other words, true wisdom does not only make us wise, but humble. While knowledge puffs up (1 Co. 8:1), one who is wise knows better than to be arrogant about his wisdom. His behavior toward others, then, is good; he treats all with esteem.

This is in stark contrast to those who consider themselves wise, and credit their wisdom to themselves. This "wisdom" is instead fueled by a heart of "bitter jealousy and *selfish* ambition." They see their "wisdom" both as a means and a justification to advance their personal agenda at other people's expense. Such "wise" ones are known not for humility, but rather for boastfulness and conceit. In a twisted way, they use their wisdom to "lie against the truth." Through their command of knowledge and charisma, they confound and confuse, leading others astray with their version of "wisdom."

True wisdom "descend[s] from above," intended by God to be a selfless benefit and blessing to others. But the arrogant "wisdom" that results in jealousy and ambition is instead "earthly, physical, demon-like." This "wisdom" concerns itself only with worldly accomplishments and achievements. It is self-serving—a perversion against God's gift—and is only base and evil in its output.

Indeed, while true wisdom brings order to chaos, inspiring good and godly behavior, the presence of jealousy and selfish ambition in "earthly" wisdom incites "disorder and every evil practice." The mind and heart of wisdom become corrupted, and the gift that was intended for good instead sees others as enemies and obstacles. The apparent ability to understand things from God's perspective is used as an advantage over others. The ensuing confusion this "demon-like" wisdom creates manipulates situations and people for its own gain—and no one is the wiser.

True wisdom—"the wisdom from above"—is only ever pure in its motives. It is not envious, but a seeker of peace. It is not evil in its superiority, but gentle in the use of its godly gift. True wisdom does not desire control, but looks for ways to cooperate and work together with others. It is full of loving-kindness, not arrogance; it is uncontentious, not combative; it is unhypocritical, not deceptive.

The wisdom that God bestows on us, then, is not evidenced by how much or what we know, but on our ability to apply His wisdom without allowing our flesh to corrupt it. The wisdom from above is pure, producing humility and goodness; earthly wisdom is selfish, breeding envy and ambition. Which wisdom will you wield?

QUESTIONS

Chapter 15

1. If we desire to be wise, it is crucial for us to understand what that really means. According to the chapter, what are some of the ways that people often define *wisdom?* How do these definitions compare to the description of true wisdom given by Ya'aqov?

2. Ya'aqov warns against wisdom that "is not descending from above, but *is* earthly, physical, demon-like." What are the defining characteristics of such earthly wisdom? Explain how this type of wisdom results in "disorder and every evil practice."

3. Wisdom and understanding are not proven by what or how much we know, but by our actions—by the way we put our wisdom to use. What are the defining characteristics of "the

wisdom from above?" When you act with this type of wisdom, what kind of results should you expect?

4. Take a moment to evaluate the quality of your own wisdom: How often do you show yourself to be wise and understanding? What type of wisdom are you more likely to display—earthly wisdom, or wisdom from above? What changes do you need to make in order to grow in true wisdom?

PRAYER

I praise You, ADONAI, for the goodness and wisdom You generously bestow from above. Fill me up, O God, not with knowledge and insight, but with Your heavenly mind of purity, gentleness and truth. Teach me, Father, to testify of Your wisdom through good behavior and through kind and humble acts. Master, let me not be contentious and corrupt through the wisdom of the world, but make me wise with Your wisdom and in the ways of righteousness, selflessness and peace.

Chapter 16

You Receive Not, Because You Ask Evilly

> From where *do* wars and from where *do* fightings among you *come? Are they* not from that place *created* by your passions—which are like soldiers *at war* in your *body's* members? You desire, but you do not have, *so* you murder; and *you* are jealous, and are not able to get *what you want, so* you fight and war. But you have not, because of your not asking; *or* you ask, and you receive not, because you ask evilly—so that you can spend *IT* on your pleasures.
>
> יַעֲקֹב *YA'AQOV 4:1-3 (MJLT)*

THOUGH WE AS BELIEVERS IN YESHUA are the many members of one, united Body, we nevertheless seem to have a knack for finding things to fight about. They can be petty disagreements (like over the volume or style of music in our worship services) or more serious arguments (such as disputes over doctrinal differences). Some fights are legitimate and worth having, as we confront sin or seek to defend the fundamentals of our faith. But many controversies arise out of jealousy and factions—these days, often leading to division before open confrontation ever breaks out in the first place. We just leave. Either way, infighting and unresolved conflict causes devastation and the weakening of Yeshua's Body.

Such fighting and warring comes from our *passions*—not the kind of passion that makes us *zealous* for God, but the kind that makes us *jealous* over other people. We fight (or break fellowship) with other believers when our soulish senses become offended—when we are denied support for our positions and beliefs, as we watch our opponents gain support for theirs. This kind of fighting and separation comes not because of righteousness, but because of *self-righteousness* and our selfish, fleshly reactions.

In this, we become a body at war with itself. Like an auto-immune disease that sees normal bodily functions as a foreign, invading army, we seek and destroy, no longer able to recognize friend from foe. We lash out at our fellow-sharers in Messiah—or turn our backs on them—in a futile attempt to take back what we perceive we have lost. We justify our behavior, believing we have been harmed in some way, yet our actions do nothing but deliver our mutual destruction.

We "fight and war," then, because we "desire... [what we] do not have"—favor, influence, getting our own way. And since we "do not have," and "are not able to get" what we want, we *murder* our relationships with one another—*jealous* over what others possess that we believe should be ours. Rather than sharing in each other's joy and success, we seek to steal it for ourselves.

And this reveals the reality.

The real reason we don't have what we want is not because someone else got to it first. It's not because another person has appropriated something they don't deserve that we most certainly do. And it's not a matter of being prohibited from getting what's ours while another person continues to retain what's theirs. No, the real reason we don't *have* is because we are too consumed with envy to simply *ask* for it—we are too covetous to bring it before God.

Though it's normally taken completely out of context as a remedy for meeting material needs, the fact is "you have not, because of your not asking; *or* you ask, and you receive not, because you ask evilly—so that you can spend IT on your pleasures." While elsewhere we are instructed to "ask... seek... [and] knock" (Mat. 7:7), here, the asking is tied to how we deal with our desires—our desires to receive without humbling ourselves before the Giver; our desires to spend what we acquire on our "passions" and "pleasures." Our motives are self-centered, jealous and evil.

Stop warring against yourself, gauging your wants by what other people have, and allowing strife or separation because of your own selfish envy. If you consider yourself lacking, don't let your passions rule you and foster desire and jealousy in your heart. Instead, humble yourself, be at peace with your fellow believers, and inquire of the Master with selfless motives. Don't be so self-focused that you won't ask God for what you need—just make sure you first ask Him what He wants most from you.

QUESTIONS

Chapter 16

1. All too often, fights or disagreements arise between Messiah-followers. What types of conflicts have you experienced or observed among believers? How do such conflicts affect Yeshua's Body as a whole? Are there any legitimate reasons for fights between believers? Explain your answer.

2. According to Ya'aqov, what is the true source of wars and fights among believers? When other people receive things we desire—material success, recognition and influence, positions of power, or anything else we feel should have been ours—why do we then lash out against those people?

3. How do envy and covetousness keep us from receiving the things that we want? What things have you fought to obtain

for yourself—even by trying to take them away from others—instead of simply asking God to give you those things?

4. Sometimes we ask God for things, but we don't receive them because we ask with evil motivations. Why is it wrong to ask for something "so that you can spend *it* on your pleasures"? Before you request something from God, what questions could you ask yourself to make sure that your motivations are pure?

--- P R A Y E R ---

Master Yeshua, Your judgment is just; forgive me for contributing to the senseless weakening and warring within Your Body. Give me passion, God, not for my own desires, but for Your will and the oneness of Your people. I humbly come before You, Father, to ask not for my own pleasures, but only for what I need in obedience of Your word. I praise You, ADONAI, for revealing my covetous heart, and for teaching me how to selflessly ask… and receive.

Chapter 17

Friendship Is Hostility

"Adulteresses! Have you not known that the world's friendship is hostility with God? Whoever, then, wants to be a friend of the world is made an enemy of God. Do you think that, emptily, the Scripture says *that* with envy the רוּחַ, Ruach that He caused to live in us earnestly desires *us*? But greater *unmerited* favor He gives! Therefore, *the Scripture* says, "God sets Himself against proud ones; but to humble ones, He gives *unmerited* favor."

יַעֲקֹב *YA'AQOV 4:4-6 (MJLT)*

It is written that "Adonai, whose name *is* Jealous, is a jealous God" (שְׁמוֹת Sh'mot 34:14). This righteous jealousy springs forth from the Creator's desire that His people love Him and not bow themselves to another god—that they not trade their devotions to some strange and foreign deity. His jealousy, however, is aroused neither from a place of insecurity nor codependence, but rather from a rightful possessiveness and ownership. He is jealous because He does not give away His love casually or cheaply. God's love comes at a cost that no one is able or willing to pay but Him.

It is not an exaggeration, then, to say that we are "Adulteresses!" when we give Him cause to be jealous. Just as adultery demonstrates a profound enmity toward both the loyal spouse and the foundation of the marriage itself, so also does turning toward another object of worship. The God who loves, defends and cares for us considers it to be a hostile act. To befriend another god in particular, or the ways of the world in general, is to infringe upon a sacred relationship and betray a hallowed trust. There is no such thing as an innocent intimacy with a person not your spouse; thus, "the world's friendship is hostility with God."

When we bow at the altars of materialism, entertainment, sports, politics, social media, social life, work, recreation, and even religion—to say nothing of indulgences in sin and the flesh—we are committing adultery with the world. By forsaking the covenant with our Maker, we not only call our commitment to Him into question, but we understandably enrage the lover of our soul. In choosing to augment our perfect and spiritual relationship with God by way of an imperfect, corporeal tryst with the world, we succeed not just in straining that relationship, but in making ourselves into His enemy.

Once our relationship with God deteriorates to this extent, the Ruach "that He caused to live in us," is made to "earnestly desire" us "with envy." This means that while God's troubled Ruach in us continues to endure our shameless presence, our unfaithfulness forces Him to both loathe and long for us, all at the same time. In response to our betrayal, His Ruach aches for ours, as both hostility and yearning collide. But unlike a jilted lover, the God of the universe will not reply by pining away for us, or being passive aggressive. Rather, He waits patiently, always prepared to give way to forgiveness and reconciliation.

Though we betray Him through our unsavory behavior, gratuitous amusement and worldly associations—though our unfaithfulness incites His hostility and marks us as His adversaries—our God still stands ready to hear our contrite confession. Under no obligation to take us back and invite us to repair the damage we have done to the relationship, He nevertheless permits our treachery to elicit a compassion within Himself that exponentially exceeds the degree of our disgrace. While we deserve no such kindness, and no amount of disloyalty warrants such reward, the greater our wrongdoing, the greater His forbearance—and the "greater *unmerited* favor He gives!"

To be a friend of the world—to have other "gods" before our God—is the height of arrogance, conceit and pride. It makes jealous the One who is nothing toward us but selfless; it puts our desires above Yeshua's sacrifice. Surely, "God sets Himself against proud ones," and will not be slow to envy and hostility. And yet, "to humble ones, He gives *unmerited* favor," and is quick to receive us back in forgiveness.

Have you been cheating on God with the way you spend your time, finances and resources? Humble yourself today and end your friendship with the world. Receive compassion, forgiveness and unwarranted, unmerited favor; be committed solely to the One who has been only faithful to you—and be an enemy of God no more.

QUESTIONS

Chapter 17

1. Ya'aqov harshly addresses those who pursue friendship with the world, calling them adulteresses. Explain how befriending the world violates our relationship with God in the same way adultery violates a marriage. What are some signs that would indicate a person is a friend of the world?

2. We usually think of jealousy and envy in a negative light, yet Scripture says that ADONAI is jealous (Ex. 34:14), and His Ruach "earnestly desire[s]" us "with envy." How do we cause God to be jealous or envious toward us? Why is His jealousy or envy both justified and righteous?

3. Despite our disloyalty, God desires reconciliation, and "greater *unmerited* favor He gives!" According to Ya'aqov, what determines whether God will "set Himself against" us or show

us unmerited favor (grace)? How does the world's friendship keep us from being able to receive God's unmerited favor and forgiveness?

4. In what ways have you given away and been unfaithful with things that should have been reserved for God—your time, resources, devotion, loyalty, or even worship? Knowing that the world's friendship makes you an enemy of God, what specific steps will you take in order to restore your relationship with Him?

PRAYER

ADONAI my God, I confess my unfaithfulness to You! It didn't seem like much at first, but I've clearly replaced You in areas of my heart, mind and life that should have been reserved only for You. Please forgive me, Father, for my hostile friendship with the world—how I have made You burn with jealousy over my adulterous loves. I praise You, Master, and humble myself before You, for Your unmerited favor, unwarranted compassion and unending faithfulness.

Chapter 18

Be Submitted and He Will Exalt You

> Be submitted, then, to God; stand up against the Accuser, and he will flee from you. Draw near to God, and He will draw near to you. Cleanse *your* hands, you sinners! and purify *your* hearts, you two-minded *ones!* Be exceedingly afflicted, and mourn, and weep; let your laughter be turned to mourning, and the joy to heaviness. Be made low before the Master, and He will exalt you.
>
> יַעֲקֹב *YA'AQOV 4:7-10 (MJLT)*

THE INFLUENCE OF THE ACCUSER IS INVASIVE. Given the opportunity, it uncoils within us—tempting, misleading, scheming and lying its way deep into our lives. That ancient serpent, who has the power of death, is able to gain access to us through our "hostility with God" and our complicit "friendship" with the world (יַעֲקֹב Ya'aqov 4:4-6). We are scarcely aware that the world's wooing is, in fact, such a violent assault on our souls. In the course of being so passionately pursued, we grow in pride and distance from God, being swept away not so much by an attack of the enemy as by our own failure to mount a defense. The Adversary's endgame is our destruction, accomplished through the contamination of our hearts and minds; the remedy is to actively ward off his advances, accomplished only through our *humility*.

"Be submitted, then, to God," is a straightforward resolution, yet for too many of us, this is easier said than done. Since we have created a two-front war for ourselves—between our love for the world and our enmity with the Maker—we must seek restoration to God while simultaneously stopping the Adversary's forward progress. For that, we need only to "stand up against the Accuser," and at the authority of our resistance, "he will flee from [us]."

Our tendency, however, is to either shrink from this advice, or to receive it as a call to arms. We either disbelieve in the necessity to do something about it, or we let fly all manner of fiery, spiritual warfare. Yet overcoming this snake calls for neither cowardice nor combat, but rather the unorthodox tactic of self-abasement.

Without fear or presumption, the reversal of our condition begins when we humbly "draw near to God." By taking that first step and reinitiating contact with Him, we demonstrate our grief and regret at ever having conspired with the enemy. God sees our contriteness of heart through the integrity of our actions—it softens His hostility, and restores His trust toward us—and once again He begins to extend His protection. In our drawing near to Him, "He," in turn, "will draw near to you."

Now, in the presence of His holiness, we take responsibility for our defilement: "Cleanse *your* hands, you sinners! and purify *your* hearts, you two-minded *ones!*" Acknowledging that we have been sinners—having held both the foul and the forbidden—we offer up our filthy hands in helplessness and surrender, bathing them in the waters of humility and forgiveness. Our hearts, however, have been hard—the loyalty of our minds, divided—so we must will-lessly choose full immersion in the pools of submission. Cleansed and purified, our soul is laid bare, as the remnants of the world are washed away in the purging showers of obedience.

"Be exceedingly afflicted, and mourn, and weep"—there is nothing left of us now. "Let your laughter be turned to mourning, and the joy to heaviness"—we must bear the weight of our consequences. Realizing not only the depth of our past compromise, but the hurt and sadness our unfaithfulness has inflicted upon God, we lay ourselves down to make restitution for our actions, putting upon ourselves the same affliction we caused Him. "Be made low before the Master," let Him rise to fill your self-oppression, and then—near, cleansed and humbled—"He will exalt you."

When we have truly faced our betrayal of God and been restored to His presence, no longer must we listen to the Accuser's accusations. Our past sins are gone, our guilt washed away, and the influence of the Accuser holds no sway. Return to God, and He will receive you; admit what you have done, and the Accuser will turn and run. Lower yourself before the Master... and then let Him raise you up in the glory of your submission.

QUESTIONS

Chapter 18

1. More often than we realize, we open ourselves up to the Accuser's influence through our "friendship" with the world. What is our Adversary's endgame, and how does he go about accomplishing it? Explain why submitting to God is necessary if we are to stand up against the Accuser and cause him to flee.

2. When we "draw near to God," then "He will draw near to [us]," but we still need to take responsibility for our defilement. What should we do in order to cleanse our hands and purify our hearts? Why are submission and obedience important parts of our cleansing and purification?

3. In a culture so focused on personal happiness, the exhortation to "be... afflicted, and mourn, and weep" is quite shock-

ing. What is the purpose of "your laughter be[ing] turned to mourning, and the joy to heaviness"? If we allow ourselves to "be made low before the Master," how will He respond?

4. In your own life, where has the Accuser gained access through your "friendship" with the world? What practical actions are you going to take to "stand up against the Accuser" so that "he will flee from you"? When you have truly faced your betrayal of God and been restored to His presence, what will be the result?

PRAYER

Father in Heaven, I have given the Accuser opportunity to pursue me, but today I will resist him… by submitting myself fully to Your will. I admit all I have done against You, my Master—all the two-mindedness and sin. My soul weeps and mourns over my betrayal of Your love, Abba. In humility, my God, I receive Your forgiveness; I no longer accept the accusations of the Accuser. My past is gone, ADONAI, and my guilt is washed away. Thank You for drawing near to me, as I humbly draw near to You.

Chapter 19

Speak Not, Judge Not, Do Not

> Speak not one against another, brothers. He who is speaking against a brother, or is judging his brother, speaks against תּוֹרָה, Torah and judges *the* תּוֹרָה, Torah. And if you judge תּוֹרָה, Torah, you are not a doer of תּוֹרָה, Torah, but a judge *of it*. One *alone* is the Giver of תּוֹרָה, Torah and Judge who is able to save and to destroy. But you—who are you *to be* judging the neighbor?
>
> יַעֲקֹב YA'AQOV 4:11-12 (MJLT)

IN TIMES OF TENSION AND STRESS, it is not unusual to respond aggressively to disagreement and discord. It is not unusual, but it is unhelpful, as aggression rarely yields a harmonious outcome. The words we speak to one another, then, become influenced by our distorted views of our perceived opponent. This unrighteous evaluation affects whether we deem that person worthy of our civility, honesty and respect—as if our judgment should have the power to adjust our kindness. While it may seem natural to have such a bias toward those we view as enemies, it is especially heinous when we practice this behavior with our own "brothers" and "neighbors"—when we speak against our fellow believers in Messiah.

Arguments and disputes among believers are, of course, nothing new—nor are they necessarily wrong. As human beings, believers quarrel over things common to all people; as followers of Messiah, we also enter into conflict over internal spiritual and theological matters. But while having disagreements is to be expected, speaking directly against one another makes the matter inappropriately personal. When we speak against one another, it comes not from a place of measured and sound judgment, but of unfair and unequal judgmentalism. It's when we allow the color of our perspective to influence the soundness of our judgment that we get ourselves into trouble.

The Master Yeshua teaches us not to judge each other in this way because it makes us worthy of the same poor judgment in return. If you are going to speak judgmentally against a brother, then you also deserve to receive the same inequity, for "with what*ever* measure you measure, it will be measured to you" (מַתִּתְיָהוּ Matit'yahu 7:2, MJLT). We are "speaking against" our brothers when we lie about them, or misrepresent their position, or condemn them without just cause. But we are also speaking against them when we attack them for the speck of sawdust in their eye while refusing to address the log that is in our own. Before we can legitimately confront our brother on anything, the Master says we first need to "see clearly"—and we can't do that through emotions, dishonesty, a sense of moral superiority, or any other measure of inequitable judgment.

Indeed, when we are "speaking against a brother, or… judging [our] brother," we are doing far more damage than we realize. Not only are we disparaging a family member—a member of Messiah's own Body—but we are "speak[ing] against תּוֹרָה, Torah and judg[ing] *the* תּוֹרָה, Torah." The same accusations and judgmentalism that we levy against our brother is then transferred to God's written word. We cast judgment on the Scriptures themselves, and arrogantly blame them for an insufficiency that it is impossible for them to have. When we speak against our brother, we are displacing God—we are judging according to our own subjective judgment, and not by the objective standard of Scripture—and in so doing, we fail to do that same Torah which teaches us righteousness, forgiveness, kindness and unmerited favor. We cannot at the same time be both a doer of God's word and its judge.

When we "speak against" our brother—when we judge our neighbor with aggressive, distorted, inequitable measures—we are attempting to occupy a seat that God will never vacate. We are assuming an authority to which we have no claim, for "one *alone* is the Giver of תּוֹרָה, Torah and Judge who is able to save and to destroy." No matter what wrong you may feel has been perpetrated against you, or what position you will defend to the death, it is not for you to decide whether your brother should be torn down, or if he is worthy of kindness. Only God can judge. Indeed, "who are you *to be* judging the neighbor?"

QUESTIONS

Chapter 19

1. When our perspective is clouded by tension and disagreement, we often overlook the instruction to "speak not one against another." Why does an aggressive response to conflict cause us to speak against our fellow believers? What is the difference between sound judgment and unsound judgmentalism?

2. Yeshua said that in the same way you measure judgment to others, "it will be measured to you." How does "speaking against" a brother show that we are judging with unequal measures? According to the chapter, what things keep us from seeing clearly, such that we are unable to legitimately confront a brother?

3. When we use our own subjective judgment to condemn our fellow believers, what are we saying about the Scriptures' suf-

ficiency to determine right and wrong? In what ways is judging your brother (and thereby judging the Torah) incompatible with being a doer of Torah?

4. Ya'aqov says, "One *alone* is the... Judge who is able to save and to destroy." So why do we feel justified in speaking against or judging a brother whom we perceive to be our opponent? What fellow believers have you deemed unworthy of your civility, respect, or kindness... and what are you going to do about it?

PRAYER

ADONAI my God, I praise You for Your loving-kindness—yet, with that same mouth, I've emotionally spewed judgment upon others. Forgive me, Father, for speaking and seeing through my sense of superiority and inequity, rather than the righteousness and sound judgment of Your word. In my judging, Abba, I've assumed Your authority and therefore spoken against and judged Your Torah. Teach my heart, Yeshua, that it's not for me to decide who is worthy of Your kindness... or mine.

Chapter 20

If the Master Wants, We Will Live

> Go, now, you who are saying, "Today or tomorrow we will go on to such-a-city, and *we* will pass *the time* there *for* a year, and do business, and make a profit"—*you* who do not *even* know the things of the next day! What is your life? For you are a vapor that is appearing for a little *while*, and then is vanishing. Instead of saying, "If the Master wants, we will live and do this or that," as it is, you boast in your pride. All such boasting is evil!
>
> יַעֲקֹב *YA'AQOV 4:13-16 (MJLT)*

THOUGH MUCH OF LIFE IS SPENT PREOCCUPIED BY THE NOW, in our hearts, we are always looking forward. While we may not often permit our minds to think or dream or hope too much about the future, deep inside, we live there—longing for the mended, the safer, the better. So when we do get down to deliberately planning, we plan not only for the start, but the end. We move forward—sometimes with trepidation, but most times with expectations—wishing for and predicting our happiness and success.

But even with the best laid plans—even with thorough preparation and proven strategies and a mountain of experience—we can never know with absolute certainty what will happen. Indeed, it is arrogance to think so. Yes, we can know what has worked in the past. Yes, from that, we can make reasonable assumptions about the future. Yes, we can learn from others who have gone before us. If we couldn't do these things, we could never make any plans at all. But "as it is, [we] boast in [our] pride," thinking that somehow, through our own judgment and expertise, we have adequately calculated the risks, arranged for contingencies, and ensured a favorable outcome. What we fail to recognize, however, is that our plans ultimately rely not on our own abilities and expectations, but on the things that are completely out of our control. We cannot constrain the unexpected.

So when it comes to our prospects for the future, the reality is that we "do not *even* know the things of the next day!" Not only can we not anticipate what will happen a year from now, we cannot even plan for everything that will happen tomorrow. While a routine, daily life tends to give the impression of security, the fact is that anything unexpected can happen to anyone at any time. It is a cold dose of truth—though not meant to paralyze or instill fear, but rather to empower. Knowing that safety and control are not only relative, but in large part an illusion, does not give us reason to give up and bury our heads. Rather, it is cause for adjusting our aim and modifying our self-perception.

"What is your life? For you are a vapor that is appearing for a little *while*, and then is vanishing." The sooner we acknowledge and accept our own insignificance, the more prepared for the future we will actually be. Our lives here on earth are but a wisp in time, and what we do, say and think will hold little significance outside the orbit of our own little worlds. Seeing ourselves as tiny and unimportant, then, is not for the purpose of inducing an identity crisis, but for making room in our lives for something bigger than ourselves—something that will give our miniscule, impermanent lives enduring context and meaning.

Our response, then, will not be to say, "Today or tomorrow we will go on to such-a-city, and *we* will pass *the time* there *for* a year, and do business, and make a profit," but rather, "If the Master wants, we will live and do this or that." As disciples of Messiah, we can make our plans, utilize our past experience and knowledge, and have hopes and expectations for the future. But unless and until we realize that it is all up to what "the Master wants," we will be lacking His guidance and blessing, leaving ourselves—unnecessarily—vulnerable.

"Many ARE the plans in a man's heart, but the design of ADONAI stands" (מִשְׁלֵי Mish'lei 19:21, MJLT). If our experiences should teach us anything, it's that we have no earthly idea what is coming. Our entire lives can change in a moment; and some things cannot even be imagined, much less anticipated. Don't plan your future either in arrogance or in fear—neither pridefully plowing ahead, nor timidly sheltering in place. Give God all your hopes, your plans and your life... for, as long as "the Master wants, we will live."

QUESTIONS

Chapter 20

1. All of us look to the future, whether we are making plans for our success, or simply assuming that tomorrow will bring what we expect. Why is it impossible to adequately plan for the future in a way that will ensure a favorable outcome? If the future is uncertain, what is the point of making any plans at all?

2. Ya'aqov rebukes those declaring their plans for the future, saying, "you boast in your pride." Explain how our plans and expectations for what is to come can be evidence of our pride. In what ways have you attempted to exert control over your circumstances, believing you could be prepared for all contingencies?

3. Eventually, we will all realize that our lives are only "a vapor that is appearing for a little *while*, and then is vanishing." Ac-

cording to the chapter, what is the purpose of seeing ourselves as tiny and unimportant? How does acknowledging and accepting our own insignificance make us more prepared for the future?

4. Unless all of our plans begin with "if the Master wants," we will be lacking His guidance and blessing. In your own life, what is the role of the Master's will in your preparations for the future? What steps do you need to take in order to make sure that your planning is not rooted either in arrogance or in fear?

PRAYER

Master of all things—Maker of destinies—I bless Your awesome and mighty Name. ADONAI my God, You see all ends from the beginning, knowing and offering guidance for even the tiniest moments of my existence. Teach me, Father, to plan neither in arrogance nor fear, but to confidently trust all my hopes only to You. I praise You, Abba, for You hold my future securely in Your hands. And by Your will alone will I do either this or that... and live.

Chapter 21

Do Good, or It Is Sin

> To him, then, *who is* knowing *how* to do good, but *is* not doing *it*, it is sin to him.
>
> יַעֲקֹב *YA'AQOV 4:17 (MJLT)*

SIN IS ONE OF THOSE TRICKY SUBJECTS with which we, as believers in Yeshua, have a tendency to play fast and loose. We know in our heads and hearts what is right and wrong, but when it comes to applying that knowledge to our lives, we like to lean as far as we can into the gray. It is from that compromised position, then, that Scripture can become twisted or misconstrued in our minds. This is why some believers will defend their sin by saying it's a matter of conscience, and not all so-called sin is the same. In other words, "it is sin to him" (as the Scriptures say) is actually a statement of relativity (so some of us believe), and, therefore, what is sin for you is not sin for me.

So if you believe that cursing and drinking (to inebriation) and "mature" entertainment and pre-marital relations are sin, but I don't, then it's sin for you—but not for me. For me, they are just adult decisions, and the Scriptures are either silent about them (that is, they don't explicitly address them), or can be understood in different ways. But if you see those things as wrong, then you just have a "weak conscience" (see 1 Corinthians 8), which means you shouldn't do them, because then you would be sinning.

But while such false thinking betrays not only the letter but also the spirit of the word, it finds no friend in "it is sin to him." Indeed, the immediately preceding verse says it all: "As it is, you boast in your pride. All such boasting is evil" (יַעֲקֹב Ya'aqov 4:16). It is arrogance that leads us to subvert the instructions of Scripture, and worse, to attempt to use Scripture itself to justify our subversion. Not only are we endeavoring to elevate ourselves and our own thoughts and standards above God's, but we are trying to use His own words to do it. And this leads to the actual point of the instructions that "to him, then, *who is* knowing *how* to do good, but *is* not doing *it*, it is sin to him." It is in arrogance that we repudiate the good we know, and, in so doing, it becomes sin… for us!

To begin with, neither "sin" nor "good" are left up to us to define. The knowledge of "*how* to do good" is not subjective, but rather conveyed to us by God Himself. He, Himself, is good (Ps. 25:8), as is obeying His words (De. 12:28). God's loving-kindness is good (Ps. 69:16), as is His command (Ro. 7:12), His Torah (Ro. 7:16), and His perfect will (Ro. 12:2). It is good to speak a word in season (Pr. 15:23), and it is good to seek justice and correct oppression (Is. 1:17). God "has declared to you, O man, what *is* good: …to do judgment, and love loving-kindness, and to walk humbly with your God" (Mi. 6:8).

Why, then, would we not want to do the good that we know? Because we are selfish and only want to do the good that we *want*.

We desire to be unbound from our responsibility to others, and to be "free" to do as we wish. With regard to ourselves, our principles, or our circumstances, we want to be answerable to no one.

"It is sin to him," then, in no way supports or implies the idea that "what is sin for you is not sin for me." Rather, it is a warning that when we do not act on the God-given and God-defined knowledge of good, then that failure to act *becomes sin*. If you see a person in need whom you can help, but you don't, your refusal to help is sin to you. If you see your brother in Messiah faltering in his faith, but you do not offer words of edification and correction, your holding your tongue is sin to you. We know the good we are to do, and God's word tells us how to do it. But when we know that good, and yet we do not act on it, to us, simply, "it is sin."

Claiming that "what is sin for you is not sin for me" is just another way of saying, "what is truth for you is not truth for me"—both of which are undermined by the very Scripture some attempt to use to justify it. The good we all know as Messiah-followers is the same good God has revealed in His word to us all. We have no valid reason not to do that good, and when we evade or refuse to do it, we then own that sin. "Every way of a man *is* right in his own eyes, but ADONAI is measuring hearts" (מִשְׁלֵי Mish'lei 21:2, MJLT). Don't be deceitful in dealing with others or yourself; do not sin, for you know exactly what God expects. You need look no further than the good that God has established for you. You have all you need to know... now, go do good.

QUESTIONS

Chapter 21

1. Some claim that sin is a matter of conscience, and as long as they don't feel convicted that a certain behavior is wrong, then it is not sin for them. Explain why the phrase "it is sin to him" does not support this relativistic view of sin. What role does a person's conscience play in defining sin for him?

2. Ya'aqov is speaking to those who are "knowing *how* to do good." Where do we find the knowledge of what is "sin" and what is "good"? What are some things that God calls "good"? Why is it arrogant for us to use our own thoughts and standards to determine what is "good"?

3. When we do not act on the God-given and God-defined knowledge of good, then that failure to act becomes sin.

List some motivations that would cause us to not want to do the good that we know. Why is it impossible for us to legitimately claim that we don't know the good that we should do?

4. We all need to be honest with ourselves in evaluating whether or not we are doing the things that we know are good. In your own life, what good have you known you should do, but you haven't done it? Knowing that it is sin to not do the good that you know, what changes and/or repentance do you need to make?

PRAYER

God in Heaven, You are so good! I praise You for the goodness of Your word, Your will, and Your over-abundant loving-kindness. But I have been arrogant, Father, having denied and unequally applied the truth, believing that sin is in the eye of the beholder. Forgive me, Master, not only for misusing Your word, but for sinning through my failure to do what I know is good. Convict my heart of the fullness of Your goodness, ADONAI, that I may always know and only do Your good.

Chapter 22

You Stored Up Treasure

> Go, now, you *who are* rich! Weep, howling over your miseries that are coming upon *you*! Your riches have rotted, and your garments have become moth-eaten. Your gold and silver have corroded, and the corrosion of them will be to you for a testimony, and will eat your flesh like fire. You stored up treasure *for yourselves, as if we were not* in the last days! Look! the wages of the workmen (...which had been fraudulently withheld by you) cry out.... You lived in luxury upon the earth, and were self-indulgent; you fed your hearts in a day of slaughter....
>
> יַעֲקֹב *YA'AQOV 5:1-6 (MJLT)*

BY NOW, IT MAY BE A LAUGHABLE STATISTIC: the "good old days," when the U.S. national debt was *only* $30 trillion—of which the debt per tax payer was *merely* $250,000. This, of course, does not even seem real—it is literally unfathomable—given that the average American has enough trouble with his share of our collective personal debt (mortgages, credit cards and such) totaling $15 trillion. With such a heavy weight, then, it is understandable for us to see the accumulation of wealth as a way out—a rescue from a mounting and unsustainable deficit. But what if achieving financial security is not the answer? What if being rich is actually more risky than simply having enough?

It is difficult to convince a rich person that he is destitute. Indeed, even someone who lives in any amount of comfort will not honestly assess himself as impoverished, though he may still consider himself lacking. Yet the way we view and use our wealth can signify that we are actually quite bankrupt—and not because we are all out of money.

Though "a root of all the evils is the love of money" (1 Timothy 6:10, MJLT), we do not become bereft through wealth simply as a consequence of having it. When we are rich (or comfortable), we continually look to have greater affluence (or more comfort), and to hold onto our wealth so that our standard of living might be increased—or at minimum, maintained. But this obsession for our provision today—even for tomorrow—is short-sighted, because, as we well know, riches do not last forever. We forget that while we seek to solve our seemingly unending problems with money, the solution of wealth is only temporary. The misery from riches, then, comes not from the wealth itself, but from our mistaken misperception of its enduring solvency.

We pretend that money holds its value and economies can't collapse, but if they do, a bailout from thin air is just an electronic bank deposit away. Even for those who actually plan for the worst, sensing that it is only a matter of time, gold and silver will yet corrode (their prudent preparedness notwithstanding). Obviously, money can and often does improve our lives, and both saving and being fiscally responsible are righteous deeds. But wealth becomes a problem because it becomes our god—we look to it as the source of our daily provision, and we trust in it for our ongoing protection, expecting it to take care of us. Such riches "have rotted" and "become moth-eaten"; they "will eat your flesh like fire." A salvific approach to money—no matter how well-intended—is nothing short of worship… a savior set up in the place of God.

The more we look to wealth to rescue us, the more vulnerable we also become to the lure of luxury and self-indulgence. When our needs start being met, and we credit money for the relief, our eyes begin to wander from needs to wants—and soon we are fattening ourselves up for "a day of slaughter." Even if we give a portion of it away, letting others benefit from our increase, as long as our undertone is one of self-preservation, we are acting "*as if we were not in the last days,*" placing our hope in a destructible store.

We demonstrate our spiritual bankruptcy by counting on money to rescue us from our circumstances, and finding financial security in our bottom line, rather than investing our faith in the eternal provision of Yeshua. When we feed our hearts with the confidence and comfort of money, it robs us of our reliance upon the only one that is truly imperishable. One day, all things will pass away, and any amount of wealth we accumulate will be made worthless. Don't let the miseries of riches come upon you, but store up your trust in the treasure that truly lasts forever.

QUESTIONS

Chapter 22

1. In a culture overwhelmed by debt, it's easy to view the accumulation of wealth as the answer to our problems. Why is money unable to offer the lasting solution we seek? How can a rich person—or even someone with just a moderate level of financial comfort—actually be impoverished or destitute?

2. Preparing for the future and being fiscally responsible are both righteous actions, yet money has no real power to save us. Explain how putting our trust in wealth ultimately becomes a form of idolatry. What are some proper attitudes we should have as we practice good financial stewardship?

3. Ya'aqov has extremely harsh words for the rich—those who "stored up treasure *for [them]selves, as if we were not* in the last

days!" In what ways can wealth lead us into sin, such that we take things for ourselves even at the expense of others? How should being "in the last days" affect our perspective on wealth?

4. One day, all things will pass away, and any amount of wealth we accumulate will be made worthless. Describe the confidence you have for the future, and why you have good reason for that confidence. Which things that you currently value will not endure? What treasures are you storing up that will last forever?

PRAYER

I praise You, ADONAI, and bless You in Your bountiful greatness. You alone sustain me, whether in my abundance or my lack. Teach me, Master, not to be short-sighted in my pursuit of comfort and wealth, believing that poverty may be solved merely through the making of money. Humble me, Master, and show my heart that without You I will never be anything but destitute. You alone, O God, are my inheritance and my salvation; help me to remember to invest all of my treasure in You.

Chapter 23

Be Patient and Stabilize Your Heart

> Be patient, then, brothers, until the *coming* presence of the Master. Look! the farmer awaits the precious fruit of the earth, being patient for it until he receives rain—יוֹרֶה וּמַלְקוֹשׁ, Yoreh uMal'qosh. You also, be patient; stabilize your hearts, because the *coming* presence of the Master has drawn near.
>
> יַעֲקֹב *YA'AQOV 5:7-8 (MJLT)*

ANYTIME, GOD. IN FACT, RIGHT NOW WOULD BE GOOD. It's getting kind of hairy down here, and a bunch of us are starting to feel just a tad bit uneasy. Yep. Getting a little too close for comfort, if You know what I mean. So, what do You say, Lord? How about You come back for us now? We are totally ready for You, I promise. Even if we have to stretch it to next Tuesday, I think that could still work for everybody, right fellas? Obviously, God, it's up to You, and You probably know best and all, but seriously—and I mean this with all sincerity—*this place is nuts! Get me out of here! Help! Help! Heeeelp!*

As we near the end of all things, and the intensity of this mortal life continues to increase, it is understandable to feel that we've reached the point (or we've passed the point) that it's time to go. It can make us antsy that Yeshua appears to be keeping us waiting, especially when it seems we are closer to the edge than humanity has ever been. Of course, it could just be our limited perspective. After all, they're not throwing us to the lions... yet. But while we wait for the Master's inevitable—albeit seemingly overdue—return, we have to look at it from His point of view.

Though it is reasonable to wonder just how much more we can possibly take, we need to keep in mind that we're not the only ones waiting. It often appears to us as if ADONAI is being "slow in regard to the promise" of Yeshua's coming, though He is, in fact, "not slow" at all, but rather "is patient toward you" (כֵּיפָא ב 2 Keifa 3:9, MJLT). He is taking His time (from our perspective) not for some arbitrary reason, but for our collective soul. Indeed, though the gate leading to Life is narrow—and the road is tight, and few will ever find it (מַתִּתְיָהוּ Matit'yahu 7:14)—God nevertheless wishes none to be lost, but for all His creation to reform.

Yeshua will return, then, just as is promised... but not a second sooner than the moment He can wait for us no more. The presence of the Master will indeed come. So while we work and we wait, we must trust and believe and *be patient.*

Consider the farmer who plows his field and plants his seed, but then must wait for the rain—and then wait again for the earth to bear its fruit. What is the use of questioning the sky, or asking the ground to hurry up? Nothing in the farmer's experience tells him that, as long as the elements cooperate, his crops will fail to yield a harvest. He therefore believes—he expects—his labors to bear fruit in the due course of time. He has no reason to doubt what has never let him down.

So too must we trust Yeshua to come and save us from this mess in His perfect time. Are we not laboring for God? Are we not plowing His fields and planting His seed? If we do not fail in these things, then all that is left is to wait for the rains. They will fall or be withheld according to the hand and will of God. But if we trust Him with our eternity, surely we can trust Him with our today.

Like the farmer, then, "be patient" and "stabilize your hearts." Don't allow the times to toss you about and break you down—to demoralize you and mislead you such that you doubt He will ever really come. Just remember that even as you wait for Him, He is waiting for us, and allow that truth to bring patience and stability to your heart.

Whether in good times or in evil, our heart's desire should always be Heavenward. So while we wait for the Master to retrieve us, we must keep doing His work no matter the cost—caring for people, raising our children, proclaiming the truth, fighting for what is right.... Be patient and stable in heart, and worry not for what is coming against us tomorrow. Trust Yeshua now with your today, "because the *coming* presence of the Master has drawn near."

QUESTIONS

Chapter 23

1. As we watch the state of the world rapidly deteriorate around us, sometimes it seems as if Yeshua's return is taking too long. What concerning things are currently taking place that make you feel like the end must be near? How do these things compare to what previous generations have endured?

2. Although we might think that ADONAI is being "slow in regard to the promise" of Yeshua's return, His perspective is different from ours. Read 2 Keifa (Peter) 3:9. Why is God patiently waiting to fulfill His promise? How does it make you feel to realize that He is being patient toward us?

3. To illustrate the type of patience we should have, Ya'aqov uses the analogy of a farmer who patiently waits for the earth to

bear fruit. Why does the farmer trust that the rains will come at their appropriate times? Explain how we can have this same kind of trust as we wait for Yeshua's coming.

4. While we wait for "the coming presence of the Master," we need to stabilize our hearts and keep doing His work. What specific work do you, personally, need to be doing for the Master as you await His return? How can you stabilize your heart so that you will be able to persevere with patience and hope?

PRAYER

Come quickly, Master Yeshua! Your people eagerly anticipate Your return! But while we wait, ADONAI, please fill me with Your patience, that I may endure in confidence and righteousness to the end. I bless Your Name, O God, and praise You; help me to trust You for my today as much as I count on You for my tomorrow. Stabilize my heart, Father, that I may no longer be tossed about by the world around me, but instead persevere and find balance, strength and hope in the promise of Your soon, coming presence.

Chapter 24

Thou Shalt Not Grumble

> Do not grumble against one another, brothers, so that you may not be judged. Look! the Judge is standing at the door! *As* an example, brothers, of the suffering of evil and of the patience, take the prophets who spoke in the Name of ADONAI. Look! we call happy those who were enduring *with* the perseverance of אִיוֹב, Iyov—*which* you *have* heard of—and you have seen ADONAI's goal: that ADONAI is very compassionate and merciful.
>
> יַעֲקֹב *YA'AQOV 5:9-11* (MJLT)

YOU'VE BEEN GRAVELY WRONGED. Or, perhaps, not wronged, but definitely deeply offended. Or maybe not so much offended as frustrated or inconvenienced or mildly bothered in general. But they surely have it out for you, and they're doing it to you on purpose! Or, perhaps, not on purpose, but they're definitely being incredibly selfish. Or maybe not so much selfish as neglectful or forgetful or just plain oblivious. Well, they've got another thing coming! You're going to give them a piece of your mind! Or, perhaps, not give them a piece of your mind, but definitely complain about it to someone not directly involved. Or maybe not complain about it so much as moan and groan and grumble about it... to yourself.

When we "grumble against one another," it's generally because we believe some kind of wrong or offense has taken place. But rather than trying to work it out—whether because we feel there is nothing that can be done to fix the problem, or because we have a primal aversion to confrontation, or because, deep down, we're just using the issue as an excuse to gripe—we moan and groan to anyone who will listen... especially in our hearts.

Grumbling, then, is more than complaining. Warranted or not, outward or not, to grumble is to criticize, to accuse... to judge. Our grumbling is a response to a judgment we are making about another person—about their reasons, their motives, and their intentions. We should not be surprised, then, that we are sternly advised not to grumble against others; otherwise, "you may... be judged." Indeed, as the Master teaches us, "in what*ever* judgment you judge, you will be judged, and with what*ever* measure you measure, it will be measured to you" (מַתִּתְיָהוּ Matit'yahu 7:2, MJLT). When we judge others in our grumbling, we are also bringing judgment upon ourselves.

To grumble against another person is easy; what is difficult is to endure a real or perceived hurt through perseverance and patience. "*As* an example... take the prophets" and their "suffering of evil." Elijah persevered through the persecutions of Ahab and Jezebel, enduring droughts and stretches of hiding in the desert. Daniel waited on God while also waiting for the consequence of his prayerful civil disobedience; and again he waited, facing certain death, sentenced to the lion's den. And Jeremiah, worse than his imprisonment in a cistern of sinking mud, suffered the calling of a prophet to a people who refused to listen. These all patiently bore the hardships set against them, not grumbling, but counting on God to relieve them.

Consider also "the perseverance of אִיּוֹב, Iyov—*which* you *have* heard of." He lost all his children and everything he had, yet could still say, "Will we receive the good from God, but not receive the evil?" (אִיּוֹב Iyov 2:10, MJLT). Though Job questioned God, he nevertheless remained true to the Holy One. In the face of unimaginable suffering, this one "we call happy."

Rather than grumbling, we need to endure suffering with graciousness toward those against us—we must strive toward "ADONAI's goal," which is to be "very compassionate and merciful." The Master teaches us to be "merciful, as your Father is also merciful; and judge not, and you will not be judged" (Luke 6:36-37, MJLT). When we rely on God's patience and mercy, yet deny the same to others, we become worthy of harsh, divine judgment (see Romans 2:3-5).

No matter how you feel about someone, and no matter how much hurt or offense or animosity you have received from them, grumbling—and judging through your grumbling—is not the godly answer. Instead, seek to share with them God's goal; endure, be patient, and show compassion and mercy. Don't put yourself under judgment in your grumbling against others. "Look! the Judge is standing at the door!"

QUESTIONS

Chapter 24

1. When we have been offended or wronged, we often grumble and complain—either to others or to ourselves. What kinds of "wrongs" cause us to grumble against other people? List some reasons we might continue to grumble about someone instead of trying to resolve the issues we have with them.

2. According to Ya'aqov, we should not grumble against one another "so that [we] may not be judged." In what way is grumbling more than just complaining, but actually a form of judgment? How do Yeshua's words in Matit'yahu (Matthew) 7:1-2 apply to a person who grumbles against others?

3. The prophets and Job are examples of those who suffered greatly at the hands of others, yet endured with patience and perseverance. How do the things those men went through compare to the things that cause us to grumble against one another?

What effect should remembering their example have on our own behavior?

4. "You have seen ADONAI's goal: that ADONAI is very compassionate and merciful." What compassion and mercy have you received from ADONAI? Did you deserve what you received? Knowing that "the Judge is standing at the door," how are you going to change the way you respond to being offended or wronged?

--- PRAYER

O God, I've been so hurt—at least, it sure feels that way. But I don't let on, not even to myself, and instead grumble against the object of my offenses. Help me, Father, to persevere through my suffering, and—rather than returning judgment for injury—to reflect only Your compassion and mercy. Teach me patience and graciousness toward others, ADONAI, that I may endure all harm —both real and perceived. I praise You, Yeshua, and bless Your holy Name, for showing me that it's better to be godly than to grumble.

Chapter 25

Let Your Yes Be Yes

> But before all things, my brothers, do not swear—neither "by the heaven," nor "by the earth," nor by any other oath —but let your "Yes" be "Yes," and the "No" *be* "No," so that under judgment you may not fall.
>
> יַעֲקֹב *YA'AQOV 5:12 (MJLT)*

IS IT EVER OKAY TO SWEAR? Not "swear" as in using profanity or foul language (Ephesians 4:29), but as in taking an oath, vow or pledge. Scripturally speaking, to swear is to make a kind of promise. But here, the Scriptures say, "do not swear," and, immediately, the matter becomes confusing. Are we never to make promises? Should we reject all oaths and pledges—like the Pledge of Allegiance? Are we permitted even to speak the promises of our wedding vows? When someone asks for or expects our commitment, are we to simply smile angelically and assure them noncommittally, "If the Lord wills"? Is that really what is at issue here? "Do not swear" seems to be a relatively straightforward command, but there's definitely more to the story. And if we can't understand what it takes to make a commitment, then we can't understand what it means to follow Messiah.

To understand swearing, we first have to accept that God Himself swears. Luke 1:73 (cf. Ge. 22:15ff) explicitly tells us that He took an "oath that He swore to אַבְרָהָם, Av'raham our father" (MJLT). He also expressly swore to David (Ac. 2:30, Ps. 132:11) and to Israel (He. 3:11, Ps. 95:11). When God "swore by Himself" to Av'raham (because there was "no *one* greater" by which to swear), the Scriptures point to this as the reason why—and the conditions under which—oaths between people become binding. In other words, an oath settles a matter when "men swear by the *one* greater *than themselves*" (עִבְרִים Iv'riym 6:13ff, MJLT)—that is, God.

This is precisely why, when we testify in court (in some jurisdictions), we swear under oath that our testimony is true, "So help me God." Such an oath is intended to give weight to the veracity of the testimony, binding the witness to the command to "not swear to falsehood by My Name" (וַיִּקְרָא Vayiq'ra 19:12, MJLT). By invoking God's name, we risk profaning His character and bringing guilt upon ourselves (Ex. 20:7, De. 23:21). Therefore, unless we are willing to incur such a cost, we are highly motivated to tell the truth.

So to the matter of "do not swear," it seems that Scripture actually endorses what it appears to be forbidding. In fact, Ya'aqov's injunction to not swear "by the heaven" is made even more confusing by Yeshua's own statement that "he who swore by the heaven swears by the throne of God, and by Him who is sitting upon it" (מַתִּתְיָהוּ Matit'yahu 23:22, MJLT). An oath in God's name, then, is not only binding, but the *correct* way of making an oath, according to Yeshua. But how can an oath that we are not allowed to swear—by a heaven that we are not supposed to swear by—be acceptable, much less legitimate?

This tension is resolved when we realize that Ya'aqov is actually expounding upon בְּמִדְבַּר B'mid'bar 30:2, "When a man vows a vow to ADONAI, or has sworn an oath to bind a bond on his soul, he must not break his word" (MJLT). What he is telling us to avoid, then, is not swearing oaths and vows altogether, *but breaking our word*—that we should not make oaths and vows when our word ought to be enough. This is what Yeshua is also saying with a directive nearly identical to that of Ya'aqov: "[do] not... swear at all; neither by the heaven... nor by the earth... [nor] by your head.... But let your word be, 'Yes, yes,' *or* 'No, no,' and *anything* which is more than these is of the evil" (מַתִּתְיָהוּ Matit'yahu 5:33-37, MJLT).

In every commitment, then, we must not put on an elaborate verbal show in the hopes of convincing others of our integrity. Rather, we are expected to keep our word whether we swear to it or not. When you say you will do something ("Yes, yes"), just do it. And when you say that you won't ("No, no"), don't—otherwise, "under judgment you [will] fall." If you are committed to following Yeshua and being His representative, don't tarnish either His reputation or yours by breaking your word. Make promises and then keep them. Think before you speak, be precise, and don't obfuscate. "Before all things," let your word be your bond, telling nothing but the truth... so help you God.

Is it ever okay to swear? Well, yes and no.

QUESTIONS

Chapter 25

1. "Do not swear" seems like a straightforward command, but there is definitely more to it—since God Himself swears. Biblically speaking, what does it mean to swear? List some situations in which a person would swear an oath or vow. What is the purpose of invoking God's Name when swearing?

2. When a person swears in God's Name, it should cause him to be highly motivated to tell the truth. If we swear an oath and invoke God's Name, what are we risking? Outside the context of formal commitments, what might cause someone to regularly feel the need to swear oaths in his daily life?

3. In their teachings about swearing, Ya'aqov and Yeshua are not forbidding oaths and vows altogether, but are expounding on

the Torah. Explain what they are telling us to avoid when they instruct us not to swear. If followers of Yeshua don't keep their word at all times, how does that affect the Master's reputation?

4. According to Ya'aqov, you must "let your 'Yes' be 'Yes,' and the 'No' *be* 'No,' so that under judgment you may not fall." When you say that you will or will not do something, do others trust that you will keep your word? Why, or why not? What steps do you need to take to improve the credibility of your word?

──────── PRAYER ────────

I praise Your awesome Name, ADONAI my God; in heaven and on earth, there is no one greater! May I do nothing in word or deed, Master, that could ever smear Your irreproachable reputation. Convict my heart, Father, that I may not make empty commitments—that as Your child, my word will always be my bond. I pledge my allegiance to You, Yeshua, and to speak nothing but the truth. In fear and trembling—by Your holy throne—I swear.

Chapter 26

You Are Not Alone

Does anyone suffer hardship among you? Let him pray. Is anyone *of you* cheerful? Let him sing melodies *of praise*. Is anyone infirmed among you? Let him call for the זְקֵנִים, z'qeniym of the Called-Forth, and let them pray over him, having anointed him with oil, in the Name of the Master. And the prayer of the faith will save the distressed one *from his affliction*, and the Master will raise him up...

יַעֲקֹב *YA'AQOV 5:13-15A (MJLT)*

FOR ALL OUR CONNECTIVITY THROUGH the wondrous advancements of technology, we are more separated now than we have ever been. Though we can travel half-way around the world in less than a day, or instantly see and speak to one another screen-to-screen from opposite sides of the planet, in the ways that really count, we too often find ourselves alone. These modern conveniences ironically keep us quarantined—unmotivated to even drive across town for anything mildly inconvenient. We also use technology to keep us segregated in our politics and religion, and to shelter us from the prying eyes of judgment and accountability. And the loneliness this creates, though generally not the intended result, is often deliberate and self-imposed. We grow accustomed to thinking and being by ourselves, and the distance carries over into the way we relate to God.

It is no wonder, then, that we need to be reminded to *pray* whenever we suffer hardship. It is too easy to retreat into ourselves in the vain hopes of escape, rather than reach out for comfort and help. The flesh does not understand that the act of making ourselves even more vulnerable by opening up to God in prayer not only holds the promise that He hears us, but also has the potential to ease our pain. When we see ourselves as being contained by the limits of our own abilities and happenstances, we cut ourselves off from the uncontainable, limitless God who awaits our drawing near to Him. In prayer, the first hardship we alleviate is loneliness.

So also does our aloneness affect our *praise* to God—or, rather, our lack of it. When we are "cheerful," we tend to treat that feeling more as a respite from our struggles than as a reason to praise God. Life takes a toll, while praise takes effort—though true praise is closer to effortlessness. But when the struggles seem to just keep stacking up, a cheerful situation can feel like nothing more than a break in the storm, making that momentary victory merely about ourselves. Rather than sharing that joyful moment with the Maker—by opening our mouths in songs of praise—we keep it to ourselves, and forget to connect the meeting of our needs with His desire to provide.

But there is perhaps no greater separator—both between people, and between us and God—than when we are sickly and *infirmed*.

While there may be some ailments that are sufficiently mild, requiring no significant treatment or attention, we were not created by God to convalesce alone. Especially when it comes to sudden, severe *sickness* or debilitating chronic *illness*, our chronic *loneliness* tells us to isolate and withdraw. But in denial of that instinct, we must instead reach out in our weakness and invite not only the healing power of Messiah, but also the prayers and anointing from His Called-Forth-Community. Faceless pharmaceuticals and physicians who barely know our names are not necessarily the most effective remedy we should seek. The spiritual and physical presence of those who love Yeshua and trust Him as our healer is one of the most precious healing balms of all.

"The prayer of the faith will save the distressed one *from his affliction*" because it brings us closer to God and keeps us from suffering alone. Apart from God, life's troubles leave us distressed and defined by the incidents that afflict us. But when we pray (or praise) in faith—not doubting, or figuring the odds, or preparing our hearts for nothing to happen—it saves us from the lie that we are on our own.

God is there for us—as we should be for others—so there is never a need to suffer alone. We must get out of our heads, get over ourselves, and call for help whenever we need it. In times of distress, affliction and even cheerfulness, don't forget to reach out and reconnect to God. In faith, lift up your prayers and praises to Him, believing "the Master will raise [you] up." For you are not alone.

QUESTIONS

Chapter 26

1. Despite all our technology that is designed to connect us, today's society is overwhelmed by loneliness. How do things like personal devices and social media actually contribute to our feelings of isolation? In what ways have you personally experienced loneliness or isolation?

2. As we become accustomed to isolation and loneliness, the distance we create can also affect the way we relate to God. Why do we need to be reminded to pray when we are suffering hardship? How does reaching out to God in prayer affect our perspective and begin to change our situation?

3. Ya'aqov says that anyone who is cheerful should "sing melodies *of praise*." When we are isolated and self-focused, why do we tend to overlook opportunities to joyfully give praise to God? If we fail to share our joyful moments with the Maker by

opening our mouths to praise Him, what do you think will be the result?

4. There are few things that bring greater isolation than serious illness—whether sudden or chronic. When we are sick, why is it so important to overcome our instinct to withdraw, and instead reach out for prayers and anointing from the Called-Forth-Community? How can we combat the lie that tells us we have to suffer alone?

PRAYER

Healer of the lonely, I praise You, O my God. I have conditioned myself to embrace the isolating devices of life. I have forgotten that in all my loneliness, You have never once left me. Teach my heart and mind, ADONAI, that no matter how alone I may physically be or emotionally feel, I must never neglect to reach out to You—whether in distress or in cheer. Restore me in every possible way, Yeshua, and save me from my affliction! Raise me up, Holy Savior, as I pray in vulnerable, unisolated faith.

Chapter 27

That You May Be Healed

> ...and if [the distressed one] has committed sins, they will be forgiven to him. So be confessing *your* sins to one another, and be praying for one another, *so* that you may be healed; *for of* great power is a prayer from a righteous man—working *effectively*.
>
> יַעֲקֹב YA'AQOV 5:15b-16 (MJLT)

WHENEVER WE ARE FACED WITH HARDSHIP AND DISTRESS, we know that "the prayer of the faith will save" us (5:15a)—that in our suffering and sicknesses, "the Master will raise [us] up" (5:15a), especially if we call to others for prayer (5:14). And because God patiently waits for us to reach out to Him for help, we are only alone for as long as we choose to be. But what if our need is more than just physical or circumstantial? Suppose that there is something deeper within us—something intangible and hard to get hold of —that remains unresolved even after the help comes? What if we are sometimes the cause of our own continued difficulty and pain? What if that cause is our *sin*?

To set our minds at ease, we can be assured at the outset that when we are afflicted, and we pray to God in faith for relief, "if [we have] committed sins, they will be forgiven." God does not put conditions on His forgiveness beyond the expectation of our humility and intentions to reform. Rather, because "the blood of יֵשׁוּעַ, Yeshua... cleanses us from every sin, [He is] faithful and righteous that He will forgive us" (א יוֹחָנָן 1 Yochanan 1:7-9, MJLT). God freely forgives sin as part of the contract He made with us when we accepted the Master's terms of service.

And yet, forgiveness is not the end of what remains available to us. If all we do is receive that forgiveness, thank God, and then move on, the thing that got us to the point of sinning in the first place is likely to return and make another attempt. Thankfully, there is something we can do to guard against it.

While forgiveness only requires God to know *that we know* what we did wrong—as we openly (even if ashamedly) admit it to Him—we are also supposed to "be confessing [our] sins to one another." The benefits of such a practice are incalculable. First, just the very thought of having to tell someone about the sin we are contemplating can be enough to dissuade us from it, and to remind us of who we are and Who we are serving. We not only want to avoid the embarrassment, but we want to stand clean before our God. Second, should we stumble into sin, the confession itself bolsters in our hearts and minds the truth of our walk with Messiah: that God forgives, that we are not alone, and that we have other Messiah-followers in our life who care about us, are looking out for us, and have our best interests at heart.

Following confession, we seal its cleansing effect when we apply the balm of "praying for one another." Confession alone merely humiliates, without reinforcing good, godly behavior. But prayer enables us to take a practical, spiritual step with our brother or sister—to assist them with the burden of temptation by helping them to lift it up in honesty before God and lay it at the feet of the Master.

The divine devices of confession and prayer were given to us so that even after the forgiveness of sins, "you may be healed." Without confession to others, and prayer received in return, sin can tend to leave an open wound, making us vulnerable—even likely—to repeat past bad behavior. But confession and prayer help us to clean out and heal that injury—to be set free not just from the sin, but from the guilt that keeps weighing us down.

Such spiritual healing comes only through confession to and prayer for one another because "a prayer from a righteous man" is "*of* great power... working *effectively.*" When we confess our sins to God, He forgives us; and when we believe, He credits our faith as righteousness (see Romans 4:5). But unless we confess our sins to one another, we miss out on a God-ordained mechanism to help us retain that righteousness *in our actions.* And only when we are righteous will our prayers be "*of* great power"—much less "working *effectively*"—and therefore bring healing.

Through the blood of His Son and the compassion of His children, our God has provided the means not just for our forgiveness, but for our inward healing. Reach out, and be distressed no more—be restored through confession and prayer.

QUESTIONS

Chapter 27

1. Beyond difficult circumstances or physical illness, sometimes hardship and distress can be caused by our own sin. How can we have confidence that God will forgive our sins when we humbly repent? And yet, what is likely to happen if we seek forgiveness, and then simply move on with our lives? Why?

2. Ya'aqov tells us that we should "be confessing [our] sins to one another." Have you ever confessed your sins to a fellow believer? If so, what happened as a result? If not, why not? List some ways that confessing our sins to one another can benefit our walk with Messiah.

3. Confession is not for the purpose of humiliation, but is one part in the process of healing and restoration. Why is "praying for one another" also an important part of this process?

What characteristics of a fellow believer could help you determine whether or not that person is trustworthy to be a confidant for confession and prayer?

4. The "prayer from a righteous man" is *"of* great power," and can bring healing to those who are in distress. In what areas do you need to grow in righteousness so that you can bring healing to others? How can you make sure that you are available to help others who need to confess their sins and receive prayer?

PRAYER

Master Yeshua, I praise Your holy Name. Your blood alone cleanses me from every sin, and You are faithful to forgive. Thank You, Father, for making me accountable to others to help me not return to my unrighteousness. I trust You, Abba, to bring me into relationship with those upright ones who can hear my confession and will pray for me. I bless Your Name, Adonai, for You do not leave me alone in my sin. Teach me to set aside my embarrassment and shame, that I may fully receive Your ways of forgiveness and—through my confession—be healed.

Chapter 28

Going Astray From the Truth

> My brothers, if any among you goes astray from the truth, and anyone turns him back, let him know that the one turning back a sinner from the straying of his way will save his soul from death—and will cover a great number of sins.
>
> יַעֲקֹב *YA'AQOV 5:19-20 (MJLT)*

FOR AS MUCH AS WE LOOK INWARDLY to appraise our progress as followers of Messiah, there yet remains a far greater purpose for us. Yes, all the self-assessment and challenging and strengthening we undergo is designed to make us better—though ultimately not just for the sake of ourselves. Our purpose is not to stay locked inside, merely seeking to perfect our personal holiness. Rather, we are to be equipped to see, and then to act as Yeshua's eyes and hands—as bearers of the truth that saves lost souls.

Why, then, do we step back even as one of our own ventures ever nearer to the edge? To say nothing of the countless souls wandering in ignorance (or running in defiance) from their Judge, what is it that keeps us from noticing, much less reacting to, the digression of a fellow follower of Messiah? Are we so blind that we do not see? Do we see, yet feign sightlessness? Do we fear they will judge and reject us for not minding our own business, and for sticking our piousness where it doesn't belong?

But the "brother [who] goes astray from the truth" has already passed his judgment and cast his rejection. His only hope of turning back, then, may be you.

The stray brother has lost his moorings. He knows what is true, but has turned away from it, going after something he somehow deems more beneficial. Somewhere along the way, he let go of the truth—either by choice or by coercion—to follow a way of unbelief, complicated by affections and circumstances. Perhaps unaware, perhaps with purpose, he has stepped over a bright line that is now ever-dulling in his sight. Though all on his own he detached from what is true, must he be made to face the lies alone?

Rather, what truth do we purport to have if it does not drive us to leave our own safety behind, and then go out to find our brother and try to bring him back? The truth of God, the truth of Messiah, the truth of the Scriptures all enjoin and obligate us to forsake our security and comfort, get up, and chase after the brother who is facing falseness. It may feel intrusive, it will often seem fruitless, but it is something we are indebted to do. Because regardless of the outcome, we have the truth, and God has authorized us to turn him back.

The potential for "turning back a sinner from the straying of his way" lies squarely in our hands. God, in His infinite power and wisdom, has allowed us this privilege and duty to make a difference in each other's lives—to participate with Him in decisions of life and death. Since the stray brother is deceived, obscuring the truth in his mind, he teeters toward his destruction. But through our own exertion of love, we may carry back to him the reality of God, and thereby "save his soul from death." What an awesome, dreadful role; what a terrible responsibility! The truth to which we are bound is fraught with eternal consequences. And yet, sometimes, God leaves it all up to us: will we give or withhold this glorious gift?

When we see our wayward brother, and then choose not to act or speak, our passivity makes us complicit in his demise. Though the Master Yeshua holds the keys to death and the grave, we share the Messiah's burden because we also bear His truth. By staying silent, we give consent to our brother's sin, and keep ourselves from becoming an urgent obstacle to his doom. But when we turn back a sinning brother from his swerving, straying ways, we save him from certain death, having "cover[ed]" and rescued him from "a great number of sins."

To be a follower of Messiah is the greatest joy and honor, for which the Master deserves all praise. But in the end, it is not for ourselves, but for emulating the selflessness He showed toward us. If you do nothing else in this life, let it be that you find that bright line and bear the saving reality of the Messiah Yeshua. Should the day ever come that your brother starts to stray, may it be *you* who turns him back to the truth—and, yes, who saves his soul.

QUESTIONS

Chapter 28

1. Self-reflection and growth in Messiah are important, but our greater purpose is to be bearers of the truth that saves lost souls. How does strengthening our own walk with Yeshua help us to fulfill that purpose? And yet, how can being solely focused on our personal holiness hinder us from reaching the lost?

2. In today's body of Messiah, people are going "astray from the truth" at an alarming rate. List some reasons why we either don't seem to notice or are unwilling to intervene when a fellow believer begins to go astray. How can we overcome the obstacles that keep us from taking action?

3. According to Ya'aqov, "the one turning back a sinner… will save his soul from death." How does this truth affect the way you view your role in the lives of other believers? If you see your brother straying toward sin, but you don't try to turn him

back, do you share any responsibility for his demise? Why, or why not?

4. As followers of Yeshua, we all have a duty to help our straying brothers turn back to the truth. When you see a fellow believer walking in sin, what practical steps can you take to try to turn him back? If another believer confronts you about sin in your own life, how should you respond?

─────── PRAYER ───────

ADONAI my God, I give You all glory and praise. Thank You for showing me the truth of Your word, that I may know You and follow You wholeheartedly all my days. Teach me, Yeshua, to not think of myself—withholding Your truth from wayward souls—but to accept the awesome risk, responsibility and honor of turning back sinners from their going astray. I humbly bow before You, my Master, for You have chosen this imperfect vessel to emulate Your perfect, selfless ways. Make me a light and a disciple for Your purposes, Father—for Your holy and perfect Name.

Glossary of Hebrew Terms

This glossary is alphabetized according to transliterated English. For simplicity's sake, punctuation has been ignored as far as alphabetizing is concerned.

Each entry includes the Hebrew, followed by its transliteration, followed either by the anglicized form of the word in parentheses, or, when warranted, by English translation or definition.

A

ADONAI

In small capital letters, this represents יהוה, known as the tetragrammaton, and commonly referred to as God's sacred name. In English, יהוה is often represented as YHVH, or YHWH. Many English bibles render it as "the LORD" in small capital letters, and sometimes, "Jehovah."

אַבְרָהָם, **Av'raham** (Abraham)

B

בְּמִדְבַּר, **B'mid'bar**

in the wilderness, "Numbers"

בְּרֵאשִׁית, **B'reshiyt**

in the beginning, "Genesis"

G

גֵּיהִנֹּם, **Geihinom**

"Gehenna"; that is, "hell"

I

עִבְרִים, **Iv'riym** (Hebrews)

אִיּוֹב, **Iyov** (Job)

K

כֵּיפָא, **Keifa**

Cephas; that is, Peter

M

מַתִּתְיָהוּ, **Matit'yahu** (Matthew)

מִשְׁלֵי, **Mish'lei**

"Proverbs"

R

רוּחַ, **Ruach**

Spirit

S

שָׁלוֹם, **Shalom**

when used as a greeting, it is an appropriate Hebrew equivalent for χαίρω, chairo, which means "rejoice" or "be well"; also, "peace" (εἰρήνη, eirene)

שְׁמוֹת, **Sh'mot**

"Exodus"

T

תּוֹרָה, **Torah**

instruction, "Law," five books of Moses; exclusive of the Talmud or Rabbinic traditions of Judaism

V

וַיִּקְרָא, **Vayiq'ra**

and he called; "Leviticus"

Y

יַעֲקֹב, **Ya'aqov**

Jacob or "James"

יֵשׁוּעַ, **Yeshua**

salvation, anglicized as "Jesus"

יִצְחָק, **Yitz'chaq** (Isaac)

יוֹחָנָן, **Yochanan** (John)

יוֹרֶה וּמַלְקוֹשׁ, **Yoreh uMal'qosh**

early rain and later rain

Z

זְקֵנִים, **z'qeniym**

"elders"; a group of older persons who carry weight with and responsibility for the community; leaders of the Called-Forth (z'qeniym) as compared to leaders of Israel (Z'qeniym)

About the Author

Kevin Geoffrey

Kevin Geoffrey, born Kevin Geoffrey Berger, is the firstborn son of a first-generation American, non-religious, Jewish family. Ashamed of his lineage from childhood, he deliberately attempted to hide his identity as a Jew, legally changing his name as a young adult. After experiencing an apparently miraculous healing from an incurable disease, Kevin began to search for God. Eventually, he accepted Yeshua as Messiah, a decision which would ultimately lead him to be restored to his Jewish heritage. Today, Kevin is a strong advocate for the restoration of all Jewish believers in Yeshua to their distinct calling and identity as the faithful remnant of Israel.

Kevin has been licensed by the International Alliance of Messianic Congregations and Synagogues (IAMCS), and ordained by Jewish Voice Ministries International (JVMI) and the Messianic Jewish Movement International (MJMI). He has been involved in congregational planting, leadership development, and itinerant teaching, but is best known as a writer, having authored nine books to date, including the *Messianic Daily Devotional* and *Bearing the Standard: A Rallying Cry to Uphold the Scriptures*. Kevin is also the editor of the *Messianic Jewish Literal Translation of the New Covenant Scriptures (MJLT NCS)*. In addition to writing about uniquely Messianic Jewish topics, Kevin's clear and impassioned teachings focus on true discipleship, radical life-commitment to Yeshua, and upholding the Scriptures as God's perfect standard.

Kevin is a husband, a father, and also the principal laborer of both Perfect Word Ministries and MJMI. He currently resides in Phoenix, Arizona with his wife Esther and their four cherished sons Isaac, Josiah, Hosea and Asher.

OTHER BOOKS BY
PERFECT WORD PUBLISHING

Messianic Daily Devotional

Messianic Mo'adiym Devotional

Messianic Torah Devotional

The Messianic Life:
Being a Disciple of Messiah

Deny Yourself: The Atoning
Command of Yom Kippur

Behold the Lamb (Passover Haggadah)

The Real Story of Chanukah

Bearing the Standard:
A Rallying Cry to Uphold the Scriptures

Messianic Jewish Literal Translation of the
New Covenant Scriptures (MJLT NCS)

That I May Gain Messiah:
A Messianic Jewish Devotional

resources.perfectword.org

1-888-321-PWMI

A ministry of Perfect Word Ministries

www.ingramcontent.com/pod-product-compliance
Lightning Source LLC
Chambersburg PA
CBHW070453100426
42743CB00010B/1597